Tom Kitchin's

Meat & Game

Tom Kitchin's

Meat
&Game

Absolute Press
An imprint of Bloomsbury Publishing Plc

50 Bedford Square   1385 Broadway
London   New York
WC1B 3DP   NY 10018
UK   USA

www.bloomsbury.com

ABSOLUTE PRESS and the A. logo are trademarks of
Bloomsbury Publishing Plc

First published 2017

© Tom Kitchin, 2017
Photography © Marc Millar, 2017

British Library Cataloguing-in-Publication Data
A catalogue record for this book is available from the
British Library.

Library of Congress Cataloguing-in-Publication data has
been applied for.

ISBN:
HB   9781472937803
ePDF   9781472937780
ePub   9781472937797

2 4 6 8 10 9 7 5 3 1

Printed and bound in China by C&C Offset

Notes
– All free-range eggs are hen's eggs and medium, unless
  otherwise specified.
– Herbs are fresh, unless otherwise specified.
– Buy unwaxed fruit if using the zest.
– Oven temperatures are given for fan-assisted ovens/
  conventional (non-fan)/gas ovens. Oven temperatures
  can deviate significantly from the actually setting, so use
  an oven thermometer to check the temperature.

Contents

I've lost count of the number of times people have asked me the best ways to prepare and cook game or meat that they've bought or been gifted. I often hear, 'I've got a couple of partridge in the freezer and I have no idea what to do with them', or 'I'd love to try pheasant, but I'm just not sure how to prepare it'.

Many people are genuinely interested in cooking and learning more about game, but, understandably, many home cooks feel a bit out of their comfort zone when it comes to the preparation.

I felt really inspired to create this book for many reasons, but, in particular, I am very passionate about showcasing how incredibly rewarding the process of cooking game and meat really is. At my restaurant, The Kitchin in Edinburgh, I love receiving meat and game in furs and feathers and relish the entire process from plucking to butchering the produce to make the most of every part, and creating a dish from start to finish. I want this book to push home cooks out of their comfort zones, to try and experiment with produce and recipes they haven't used before or are unfamiliar with, because that's when cooking gets really exciting.

Many people don't realise that cooking game and most kinds of meat is actually often much easier than it might seem – particularly when it comes to game. It's a myth that game is a posh food, enjoyed only by the rich who go shooting. Believe me, I'm not from a privileged background; I didn't grow up going on game shoots. My passion for game is simply one I have developed during my many years of training in some of the world's top kitchens. I would argue that game is, in fact, incredibly affordable, tasty and, in particular, enjoyable to cook; it's also very economical if you cook with every part of the produce. When it comes to game, the cooking process gives a real sense of achievement.

I hope this book will be the go-to-book on your shelf. I want to share my passion and some simple techniques and tips on the best ways to handle game and meat

produce. I have always loved working with the techniques involved and I've been lucky to have met some incredibly passionate and talented people during my career who have taught me how to respect the produce and make the most of it.

I fell in love with game as a young chef working for Pierre Koffmann at La Tante Claire, in London. I still remember witnessing the first grouse of the season arriving at the door – there was something almost magical about it. To then have the opportunity to continue to cook with all of the different types of game that arrived throughout the game season was incredibly inspiring. The game season in any restaurant is challenging, but so rewarding, and you can learn so much if you really respect the produce and marry it with other seasonal flavours. There's no doubt the game season presents some of the most interesting times in my kitchen year, but also the most satisfying and exciting.

The Glorious Twelfth – 12th of August – is the first day of the shooting season in this country and a particularly important day in my kitchen calendar. It's a day steeped in tradition for game lovers, chefs and, indeed, the world of gastronomy. The young grouse from the moors of Northumberland, Yorkshire and my homeland of Scotland are incredibly sought after. Many renowned restaurants throughout the United Kingdom aim to serve grouse for dinner that very day, and the same goes for restaurants in Paris and New York. I love how London's

iconic department store Harrods bring the young grouse down from Scotland by helicopter on the Glorious Twelfth, ready to be piped in to the Food Hall that day.

I hope the grouse recipes in this book will inspire more people to try cooking grouse at home, as it's one of my most treasured ingredients. At The Kitchin, and also at The Scran & Scallie, our Edinburgh gastro pub, we always head out on to the moors after lunch on the first day of the shooting season to collect our grouse. We rush back to the restaurant to pluck and prepare the birds to be ready for our guests that very same evening. Some guests book a year in advance for this special occasion. The Glorious Twelfth really does herald the start of the game season, and, soon after, other game produce becomes available.

As well as getting my hands on the very best produce, for me, it's all about seasonality, and I follow this through in everything I cook. I would never work with produce out of season and I apply this philosophy throughout my restaurants and in my home cooking. Seasonal produce always tastes so much better, and I believe cooking is all about following nature and allowing for those natural flavour marriages to happen in the cooking.

Many people carry one or two recipes up their sleeve that they use again and again, and this is understandable. In this book, however, I want to inspire home cooks to try experimenting with produce and recipes they haven't used before. Many of our friends, family and guests have shared their food memories of game with me over the years. Sometimes they've been put off trying or cooking game because, in the past, game was often hung for a very long time, so it wasn't always a dish of choice. Someone recently told me that their granny used to hang the pheasants in the shed until the guts fell out! That would surely put anyone off, but if you visit your local farmers' market or butcher, you can get your hands on some really great-quality game that is easy and enjoyable to cook and eat.

Not only do I enjoy cooking meat and game myself, I also love getting the kids involved, too. With four young boys in our house, I naturally introduced them to food and cooking at a very young age. They have always been around me when I am cooking and are used to seeing me work with produce, whether at home or in the restaurant, and they understand where their food comes from. I believe that knowing the relationship between nature and the food we eat is vital and something we mustn't shy away from.

It is incredibly important to pass on our knowledge to the younger generations, whether it's in a working kitchen or at home. I love experimenting with classic and traditional recipes and making them more accessible. I take great satisfaction in thinking about how I can maximise the flavours and modernise the classics without upsetting original methods or techniques.

The aim for this book is really to inspire you with my passion for game and meat

and introduce some new cooking methods. A lot of people turn to cooking as a form of relaxation, as they find themselves incredibly captivated in the process. The recipes in this book range from mid-week suppers to dinner party ideas, and I hope that trying some of them will give you that real sense of achievement and thrill which I get from cooking.

This book aims to show just how versatile cooking with game and meat can be. I'm sharing methods from roasting to braising and barbecuing, but also sharing some of my favourite soup and salad recipes to accompany the delicious meat and game.

The book is divided into 12 different chapters, with about eight recipes in each. It showcases some of my favourite game from woodcock and snipe to pheasant, hare, rabbit, grouse, partridge, wild duck and venison. I am also introducing you to some of my favourite recipes for cooking with beef, lamb, chicken and pork at home.

All these recipes are accessible for the home cook, though some dishes are more challenging and will be bound to push you out of your comfort zone slightly. You'll enjoy it!

Happy Cooking!

Tom Kitchin,
Edinburgh, 2017

Beef

Roast Topside with all the Trimmings

Roast beef on a Sunday is a big favourite in our house. Actually, I mean, it's the best meal of the week, and everything is important with a Sunday roast, from the beef to the Yorkshires. Roast topside is a great alternative to some of the more prime cuts. Always keep any leftovers, as they can be made into a great mid-week dish.

SERVES 4–6

2kg boneless topside of beef, tied
olive oil
8 shallots, peeled and left whole
3 carrots, peeled and chopped into
    large chunks
3 garlic cloves, peeled and left whole
2 bay leaves
2 celery sticks, cut in half
a handful rosemary sprigs
a handful thyme sprigs
3 tablespoons plain flour
300ml full-bodied red wine
750ml Beef Stock (page 278)
seasonal green vegetables, hot,
    to serve (optional)
sea salt and freshly cracked black pepper

For the Yorkshire puddings
115g plain flour
2 large free-range eggs
125ml milk
¾ teaspoon salt
4–6 tablespoons vegetable oil

For the horseradish cream
125ml whipping cream
½ teaspoon red wine vinegar
2 tablespoons freshly grated horseradish
1½ teaspoons crème fraîche
finely chopped chives, to garnish

The Yorkshire puddings can bake in the oven while the joint is resting after roasting, but the batter needs to stand for 3–4 hours before baking, so plan ahead. Put the flour in a mixing bowl and make a well in the centre. Add the eggs with half the milk and beat until smooth. Now add the rest of the milk and season with the salt and a good grind of pepper, mixing well. Set aside for 3–4 hours before baking.

The horseradish cream can also be made in advance. Whip the cream until it holds firm peaks, then add the wine vinegar and whisk quickly to incorporate. Fold in the horseradish and crème fraîche and season with salt. Cover and chill until required.

When you're ready to cook, season the joint with salt, then set aside for 20 minutes before roasting. Meanwhile, preheat the oven to 220°C Fan/240°C/Gas Mark 9.

Heat a large heavy-based roasting tray over a high heat on the hob, then add about 2 tablespoons of olive oil. When the oil is smoking hot, add the joint and sear it so it is nicely browned all over, then set aside. It might take 8–10 minutes to brown the beef, but it's important not to skimp on this stage.

Add a little more oil to the tray. When it is hot, add the shallots, carrots, garlic, bay leaves, celery, rosemary and thyme, and sauté for 2–3 minutes until the vegetables are beginning to colour and soften.

Return the joint to the roasting tray and roast in the oven for 15 minutes. Lower the oven temperature to 180°C Fan/200°C/Gas Mark 6 and continue roasting for a further 40 minutes for juicy pink meat. To check how the meat is cooked, insert a metal skewer into the thickest part for 30 seconds, then remove and place it to your lip. If the meat is slightly warm, the meat is ready to come out if you like it pink. If it is hot or very hot, the meat will be medium to well done. If it is cold, the joint needs longer in the oven.

Continued on page 16

When the joint comes out of the oven, transfer it to a large platter with a rim and set aside to rest, covered with kitchen foil, while you make the Yorkshire puddings.

Immediately, return the oven temperature up to 220°C Fan/240°C/Gas Mark 9 and place a baking sheet inside to heat up. Spoon about 1 tablespoon of the vegetable oil into each compartment of a non-stick 6-hole Yorkshire pudding tray. Place the tray on the baking sheet in the oven and heat for 5 minutes, or until the oil is smoking hot.

Quickly ladle the batter into the Yorkshire pudding tray to three-quarters fill each mould. Very quickly slide the tray on to the baking sheet and bake for 20 minutes, or until the puddings are well puffed and golden brown.

Meanwhile, make the gravy. Place the roasting tray you roasted the joint in over a medium heat on the hob and sprinkle the vegetables with flour. Mix well and stir for 1–2 minutes to cook out the flour, then add the red wine, stirring until it evaporates. Slowly add the beef stock, stirring to deglaze the pan and scrape up the tasty sediment from the bottom, then leave the gravy to bubble and thicken nicely.

Pass the gravy through a chinois or fine sieve into a saucepan and discard the flavouring ingredients. Tip in any of the juices that have accumulated while the joint is resting, then adjust the seasoning with salt and pepper. Garnish the horseradish cream with chives.

Carve and serve the beef with the Yorkshire puddings, horseradish cream and a seasonal green vegetable or two.

Steak and Kidney Pie with Roasted Bone Marrow

I once tried to take this dish off the menu at The Scran & Scallie and we had so many locals asking for it we had to put it back on by popular demand! It really is the perfect comfort food, and adding the bone marrow makes it that little bit more special. The kidneys are optional but for me they should always be added.

SERVES 4–6

800g stewing steak, well-trimmed
   and diced
200g ox kidney, well-trimmed and diced
75g plain flour, plus extra for rolling out
olive oil
100g smoked lardons
200g button mushrooms, trimmed,
   wiped and quartered
2 carrots, peeled and chopped
1 bouquet garni
1 garlic clove, crushed
1 onion, chopped
Worcestershire sauce
1 litre Beef Stock (page 278)
1 tablespoon chopped parsley
500g puff pastry, thawed if frozen
1 egg, beaten
1 bone marrow piece, 7.5cm tall
sea salt and freshly cracked black pepper

The steak and kidney filling can be made a day in advance and chilled overnight – just remember to return it to room temperature before putting it in the pie dish. Place the flour in a shallow tray and season with salt and pepper. Use a kitchen cloth to make sure the stewing beef and kidney are both perfectly dry, then toss them in the flour, shaking off the excess.

Heat a large flameproof casserole over a medium-high heat, then add a good splash of oil. When it is hot, add the stewing beef and kidney and fry until they are browned all over, then set aside to drain. You might have to do this in batches.

Wipe out the pan, then return it to the heat with a splash of oil. When the oil is hot, add the lardons and sauté until they render their fat and are coloured all over. Add the mushrooms, carrots, bouquet garni, garlic and onion with a pinch of salt, and continue sautéing for a further 2–3 minutes until the vegetables start to colour and soften.

Return the beef and kidney to the pan, along with a good splash of the Worcestershire sauce. Pour in the beef stock, adding water, if necessary, so the meat is submerged. Bring to the boil, then lower the heat. Taste and add salt and pepper, but remember the Worcestershire sauce will be salty, then cover the casserole and leave to simmer for 2½–3 hours until the meat is so tender it falls apart if you press it. Check occasionally and top up with water, if necessary. Set aside and leave to cool.

When you're ready to assemble the pie, preheat the oven to 200°C Fan/220°C/Gas Mark 7. Transfer the cooked meat, vegetables and all the sauce to a 2 litre-pie dish. Stir in the parsley.

Continued on page 19

Roll out the puff pastry on a lightly floured surface with a lightly floured rolling pin until it is roughly 2cm thick and 6cm larger all round than your pie dish. Cut a long strip of pastry as wide as the rim of the dish and, using a little beaten egg, secure the pastry on to the rim. Cut out another piece large enough to cover the pie dish. Brush the pastry strip with egg, then place the larger piece on top and press the edges together to seal, then trim with a knife. Crimp the edges with your fingers and thumb. Transfer the pie to a baking sheet and brush the surface with the beaten egg.

Cut 3 small steam holes in the centre. Place the pie in the oven and bake for 10 minutes, then lower the temperature to 180°C Fan/200°C/Gas Mark 6 and continue baking for a further 15–20 minutes until the filling is bubbling and the pastry is golden brown.

Meanwhile, season the bone marrow and place the piece on a baking tray and roast on a different shelf in the oven for 8–10 minutes, then remove and keep hot until the pie finishes baking.

When the pie comes out of the oven, leave it to stand for 5 minutes. Use a sharp knife to cut a round steam hole to the size of the bone in the centre of the pastry. Gently push the bone into the pastry and sprinkle with salt and pepper. It's now ready to serve.

Oxtail Soup with Cheese on Toast

Oxtail is a wonderful ingredient – the flavour and smell of oxtail stock is quite incredible, and it always reminds me of my time working in Ducasse's kitchen in France, where we always had a pot of it simmering away. It is one of those old-fashioned ingredients that has made a comeback and is now fashionable and fairly easy to get hold of. Once you've made this soup I'm sure you'll be making it time and time again.

SERVES 4

300g dried haricot beans
75g plain flour
4 oxtail pieces, about 250g each
olive oil
100g smoked lardons
4 onions, thinly sliced
2 carrots, peeled and chopped
2 celery sticks, chopped
5 black peppercorns
2 garlic cloves, crushed
1 tablespoon tomato purée
400ml full-bodied red wine
1.5 litres Beef Stock (page 278)
1 bouquet garni
chopped parsley, to garnish
sea salt and freshly crackled
    black pepper

For the cheese on toast

4 sourdough bread slices
50g butter, softened
2 teaspoons wholegrain mustard – I like
    to use Pommery
100g cheddar cheese, grated – my
    cheese of choice comes from the Isle
    of Mull
Worcestershire Sauce

Day 1

Place the haricot beans in a large bowl of water to cover and leave to soak for 24 hours.

Day 2

Put the flour in a shallow tray and season with salt and pepper. Pat the oxtail pieces very dry, then add them to the flour and roll them around until they are coated all over. Shake off the excess flour.

Heat a large flameproof casserole over a medium-high heat, then add a generous splash of oil. When it is hot, add the oxtail pieces and fry until they are browned all over, then remove from the casserole and set aside. You might have to do this in batches.

Add the lardons to the fat remaining in the casserole and sauté until they render their fat and are coloured all over. Add the onions, carrots and celery with a pinch of salt, and continue sautéing for 2–3 minutes until they are beginning to colour and soften. Stir in the peppercorns, garlic and tomato purée, and stir for 1–2 minutes to cook out the tomato purée.

Add the red wine, stirring to deglaze the pan, and boil until it evaporates. Add the stock and bouquet garni and bring to the boil. Reduce the heat to low, return all the oxtail pieces to the casserole and season with salt and pepper. Cover the casserole and leave the oxtails to simmer for 1½ hours.

Drain and rinse the haricot beans, then add them to the casserole and continue simmering for a further 1½ hours, or until the beans are tender and meat is tender enough to flake from the bones.

Remove the oxtail pieces from the casserole and set aside. Use a large metal spoon to skim off the fat floating on the surface. Return the oxtail pieces to the soup and set aside for reheating later if not serving immediately.

Just before you want to serve, preheat the grill to high. Toast the bread on one side. Turn the slices over, and spread the untoasted sides with butter. Rub in the

mustard, then generously sprinkle cheese all over, making sure you cover the whole surface. Pop the toast back under the grill until the cheese is golden brown and bubbling. Splash with Worcestershire sauce to taste.

While the bread is toasting, reheat the soup and adjust the seasoning, if necessary. Garnish with parsley and serve with the cheese on toast alongside.

Braised and Glazed Jacob's Ladders

I'm a big football fan and when I have the boys coming round to watch a match, they always ask for my ribs. Whether you're cooking for a football crowd or not, you can easily braise the ribs a few days beforehand or earlier on the day, so you just need to finish them in the oven just before everyone is ready to eat.

SERVES 4

4 Jacob's ladders (beef ribs on the bone), about 2kg in total
vegetable oil
1 carrot, peeled and roughly chopped
1 fennel head, roughly chopped
1 onion, roughly chopped
½ garlic head
2 tablespoons tomato purée
6 black peppercorns
4 allspice berries, lightly crushed
2 star anise, chopped
2 litres Beef Stock (page 278) or Chicken Stock (page 279)
1 bouquet garni
30g mixed seeds, such as sunflower seeds and pinenuts
mixed green salad, to serve (optional)
sea salt and freshly cracked black pepper

For the barbecue glaze
6 tablespoons maple syrup
3 tablespoons soy sauce
2 tablespoons Worcestershire sauce
4 teaspoons bourbon
4 teaspoons tomato ketchup
2 teaspoons Dijon mustard

Preheat the oven to 160°C Fan/180°C/Gas Mark 4. Rub the ribs with a little oil, then season them all over with salt and pepper.

Heat a large well-seasoned sauté or frying pan over a medium-high heat. Add the ribs and sear, turning them over a couple times, then remove from the pan and set aside.

Heat a heavy-based large roasting tray on the hob, then add a good splash of oil. When it is hot, add the carrot, fennel, onion and garlic, and sauté for 2–3 minutes until they are beginning to colour and soften. Add the tomato purée, peppercorns, allspice berries and star anise, and stir for a further 1–2 minutes to cook out the tomato purée.

Place the ribs in the in the tray, then pour over the beef stock, add the bouquet garni and season with salt and pepper. Bring the stock to the boil.

Cover the ribs and vegetables with a piece of greaseproof paper cut to fit the size of the tray, then put a sheet of kitchen foil on top, scrunching the edges to seal in the juices. Place the tray in the oven and leave the ribs to braise for 4½–5 hours until the meat is tender enough to flake from the bones.

Turn the oven temperature up to 200°C Fan/220°C/Gas Mark 7. Carefully transfer the ribs to a wire rack sitting over a shallow tray and set aside. It helps with the clean-up if you use the tray to catch drips.

Place all the glaze ingredients in a bowl and whisk together, then season with salt and pepper. Use a pastry brush to generously brush the ribs all over with the glaze. Return the ribs to the oven for 20–25 minutes, glazing every 5 minutes, until they are a dark barbecued colour. Sprinkle the ribs with the seeds for the last glazing. Remove the ribs from the oven and set aside to rest for 5 minutes covered with kitchen foil.

Roasted Bone Marrow and Girolles with Crispy Ox Tongue

This is a real chef's dish. Whole pieces of bone marrow like this are easily found in good butchers and supermarkets and they freeze really well if you want to stock up. The raw shallot and parsley garnish is important to cut through the richness of the marrow and tongue. Butchers are unlikely to sell you anything less than a whole tongue, which is OK, as the texture is best when cooked whole, but you're going to end up with much more meat than you need. Not to worry, though, as it makes excellent salads and sandwiches.

---- SERVES 4 ----

4 x 17.5cm top-cut bone marrow
olive oil
2 Parma ham slices
200g girolles, trimmed and wiped
4 quail's eggs
salt and freshly cracked black pepper

For the crispy ox tongue
1 ox tongue, about 1.5kg
2 garlic cloves, crushed
1 bouqet garni
1 carrot, peeled and diced
1 onion, finely chopped

To garnish
20 mini capers, rinsed
1 large shallot, thinly sliced
flat-leaf parsley leaves

First prepare the crispy ox tongue. Leave the ox tongue to soak in a large bowl of cold water for 2–3 hours, changing the water several times.

Drain the tongue, then place it in a large saucepan with fresh water to cover. Bring to the boil, skimming the surface as necessary, then add the garlic, bouquet garni, carrot and onion. Reduce the heat to a simmer, partially cover the pan and leave the tongue to simmer for 3–3½ hours until it is tender. As with any braised meat, a good way to check if it is tender is to use a roasting fork – stick it into the meat, and if the meat falls off easily it is cooked. Check the water level periodically and top up when necessary.

Carefully remove the tongue from the pan and when it is cool enough to handle, remove the coarse skin and any glands or excess fat and gristle. Leave to cool completely, then cover and chill for at least 1 hour before cutting into bite-sized pieces.

Preheat the oven to 200°C Fan/220°C/Gas Mark 7. Season the bone marrow pieces with salt and pepper. Scrunch up enough kitchen foil to cover the surface of a roasting tray, which will stop the bones from falling over while they are roasting. Place the bones on top and roast for 8 minutes, or until the bone marrow is cooked through. If you pierce the marrow with a small knife, there shouldn't be any resistance.

Pat the tongue cubes dry with kitchen paper and season with salt and pepper. Heat a large non-stick sauté or frying pan over a medium-high heat, then add enough oil to lightly cover the surface. When it is hot, add the tongue cubes and sauté for 2–3 minutes until they are crispy. Use a slotted spoon to transfer them to kitchen paper to drain well, then keep hot.

Add a little more oil, add the Parma ham slices and fry for 2–3 minutes until crispy. Transfer to the same plate as the tongue cubes to drain and keep hot.

Add a little more oil, then add the girolles with a pinch of salt and fry for 2–3 minutes until they are tender and the liquid they give off evaporates.

Return the tongue and ham to the pan, breaking the ham into large pieces, and mix together. Transfer the mix to a small heatproof dish and keep warm while you fry the quail's eggs.

Wipe out the pan, then heat a thin layer of oil. One by one, crack the eggs into the pan and fry until done as you like them. Transfer to a piece of kitchen paper to drain.

To serve, divide the tongue mixture among the bones and top each with a fried quail's egg and garnish with the capers, shallot and parsley.

Onglet Steaks with Hash Browns and Fried Eggs

This dish is one of the classics at The Scran & Scallie. Onglet is known as a secret cut among chefs and not many people use it, but your butcher can get it for you. The hash brown works perfectly with the steaks, or even on their own for breakfast.

SERVES 4

---

4 onglet steaks, 150g each
olive oil
30g butter
4 eggs
Wilted Spinach (page 276), to serve
sea salt and freshly cracked black pepper

For the hash browns
300g dry mashed potato (no butter, cream or milk), cooled
200g salted or corned beef, finely chopped
200g panko breadcrumbs
1 tablespoon wholegrain mustard
2 tablespoons plain flour for shaping

If you're planning to make this for breakfast, save time by mixing and shaping the hash browns up to 2 days in advance, then cover them with clingfilm and chill until required. Place all the hash brown ingredients, except the flour, in a bowl, season with salt and pepper and mix together. Lightly flour the work surface and place the mixture on top, then use a knife to cut it into 4 equal portions. Lightly flour your hands and pat the mixture into burger shapes. Set aside or chill until required.

When you're ready to cook, pat the onglet steaks dry and season with salt and pepper. Heat a large well-seasoned sauté or frying pan over a high heat, then add a splash of oil. When it is hot, add the steaks with the butter. As the butter melts, baste the steaks with it and fry them for 3 minutes on each side. I like my onglet rare, so fry them for a bit longer if you like them more well done. Remove the steaks from the pan, set aside to rest on a plate with a lip, covered with kitchen foil, while you cook the hash browns.

Heat a little more oil in the pan. Add the hash browns and cook over a medium to high heat for 3 minutes on each side, or until golden brown all over. Set aside and keep hot.

Wipe out the pan with kitchen paper, then add a little more oil. One by one, add the eggs to the pan and fry until they are done to your liking.

To serve, place an egg on top of each hash brown and season with salt and cracked pepper. Cut the steaks in half and add them to the plates with the wilted spinach. Any juices that have accumulated while the steaks were resting are delicious spooned over.

Peppered Fillet Steaks

One of the classics, this is a dish that will never go out of fashion. If you're looking for a treat or to impress someone, this is at the top of my list. Whenever I make this recipe, I look forward to the moment when the steaks get returned to the pan and covered in sauce. At that point, I just know how good the dish is going to taste.

— SERVES 4 —

2 tablespoons black peppercorns

1 teaspoon white peppercorns

1 teaspoon pink peppercorns

4 fillet steaks, about 220g each

olive oil

2 tablespoons finely chopped shallots

50ml brandy

200ml double cream

knob of butter, diced

1 tablespoon chopped flat-leaf parsley

1 teaspoon wholegrain mustard – I use Pommery

1 teaspoon brined green peppercorns, drained and rinsed

sea salt

freshly cracked black pepper, optional

Using a pestle and mortar, crush the black, white and pink peppercorns gently. Place the crushed pepper in to a sieve and shake off any excess powder, keeping just the crushed peppercorns. Season the steaks all over with the crushed peppercorns, patting them in with your hands so they stick, then season with salt.

Heat a large well-seasoned sauté or frying pan over a high heat, then add a drizzle of oil. When it is hot, add the steaks and fry them for 3–4 minutes on each side until well coloured. This should give you medium-rare meat, which is how I like my steaks, but fry them for a bit longer if you like. Set aside to rest on a plate with a rim for 5 minutes, covered with kitchen foil, while you make the sauce.

Add the shallots to the oil remaining in the pan and sauté for 1–2 minutes until softened, but not coloured. Add the brandy, stirring to deglaze the pan, and boil until it evaporates. You can flambé the pan if you're feeling adventurous, but it's not necessary. Add the cream and bring to the boil, then add the cooking juices that have accumulated while the steaks were resting.

As the sauce thickens whisk in the butter, then add the parsley, mustard and green peppercorns. Adjust the seasoning with salt and pepper, if necessary. Add the steaks to the pan and baste them in the sauce, then serve.

T-Bone Steaks with Bone Marrow Marmalade

Steak and bone marrow really is a marriage made in heaven, and by giving the bone marrow a twist and making it into a marmalade I take this dish to a completely new level. I've used T-bone in this recipe, but any cut of steak will work well. The T-bone, however, is pretty special. Beef jus is a great chef's ingredient for intense beef flavour and you can buy it in some supermarkets.

Whenever I have the chance I cook these steaks on the barbecue. Get the coals glowing and have the steaks at room temperature and the timing should be the same for juicy pink meat.

———————————— SERVES 4 ————————————

4 T-bone steaks, 350g each
olive oil
2 garlic cloves, crushed
2 thyme sprigs
2 rosemary sprigs
sea salt and freshly cracked black pepper

For the bone marrow marmalade
1.5 litres water
2 garlic cloves, finely chopped
1 bay leaf
1 thyme sprig
sherry vinegar
400g bone marrow pieces
50ml beef jus (see introduction)
2 spring onions, thinly sliced
1 tablespoon finely chopped shallot
1 teaspoon chopped flat-leaf parsley

At least 30 minutes and up to 3 hours before you plan to cook, put the steaks on a platter and rub them with a good splash of olive oil and one crushed garlic clove. Cover with clingfilm and set aside at room temperature. Put the remaining garlic clove in a small bowl with olive oil and tie the thyme and rosemary sprigs together to make a herb brush for basting the steaks with while cooking.

Meanwhile, to make the bone marrow marmalade, bring the water to the boil. Season with salt and add the garlic cloves, bay leaf, thyme and a splash of sherry vinegar. Use a small spoon or your thumb to push the marrow out of the bones.

Reduce the heat to a simmer, add the marrow and poach it for 5–6 minutes until the pieces become very soft. Use a slotted spoon to transfer the marrow to a plate lined with kitchen paper and leave to dry, then roughly chop.

Transfer the marrow to a small saucepan over a low heat. Add the beef jus, spring onions and shallot, and mix together. Add the parsley and a splash of sherry vinegar and season with salt and pepper, then set aside and keep warm.

When you're ready to cook, heat a large well-seasoned cast-iron, ridged griddle over a high heat. Season the steaks with salt and pepper and brush the rack with the garlic-flavoured oil. Place the steaks on the grill and cook for 3 minutes, then turn over and cook on the other side for 2–3 minutes for pink meat, basting with the garlic oil and herb brush. If you like your meat more well done, cook on the second side a bit longer. Set aside to rest for 5 minutes covered with kitchen foil.

To serve, divide the bone marrow marmalade among the steaks and spoon over any accumulated juices.

Pork

Roast Crisp Pork Belly and Roasted Apples with Apple Sauce

I wish I could say this was my recipe, but it's not. This recipe comes from Claire Koffmann, the wife of the legendary chef Pierre Koffmann. Her Sunday roasts are famous, but this one is by far the best. When cutting the pork belly at home, always use a serrated knife, as the skin will be so crispy a straight blade knife won't get through the crackling.

SERVES 4–6

1kg pork belly in one piece
500g rock salt
olive oil
3 apples, such as Cox or Braeburn

For the apple sauce
4 Bramley apples
50–60g sugar
50g butter
pinch of salt, or to taste

Day 1

Place the pork belly on a meat chopping board, skin side up. Using a small sharp knife, lightly score the skin, making criss-cross cuts all over. Take care not to cut into the flesh. Lightly rub rock salt all over the skin, place the pork belly in a non-reactive dish or baking try that will fit in your fridge, cover with clingfilm and chill for at least 6 hours, but ideally overnight.

Day 2

Preheat the oven 200°C Fan/220°C/Gas Mark 7 and bring a kettle of water to the boil. Remove the pork belly from the fridge, wash off the salt and rub dry with a kitchen cloth.

Place a roasting rack on top of a roasting tray and place the belly on top of the rack, skin side up. Pour the boiling water directly on to the pork belly, letting it run off the meat into the tray until it is about 5cm deep. Stand back so you don't get splashed.

Place the baking tray in the oven and roast the pork belly for 20 minutes. Lower the temperature to 160°C Fan/180°C/Gas Mark 4 and continue roasting for a further 3 hours, or until the skin is very crispy and the meat is tender enough to flake easily.

Meanwhile, to make the apple sauce, peel, core and chop the Bramley apples. Place them in a heavy-based saucepan with the sugar to taste, butter, salt and a splash of water. Stir over a low heat for 15–20 minutes until the apples start to break down. Adjust the seasoning with salt, if necessary. Set aside.

About 30 minutes before the pork is due to come out of the oven, cut each of the remaining apples in half and use a melon baller to remove the core. Immediately place them in the oven with the pork and roast for the remaining 30 minutes or until they are tender and lightly browned.

Leave the belly pork to rest for 5 minutes after it comes out of the oven, then cut into serving portions and serve with the apple sauce and apples. I always serve the apple sauce at room temperature, but it can be reheated.

Pork and Prawn Patty Broth

Pork and shellfish work really well together, and different cultures have been mixing them for generations. At The Kitchin one of the dishes I'm known for is a crispy pig's head served with roasted langoustine. On a more everyday basis, however, my wife and her girlfriends love this pork and prawn broth for their girlie nights, and you can easily add more chilli or coriander depending on how intense you like the flavour to be.

— SERVES 4 —

1 litre Chicken Stock (page 279)

1 fresh red chilli, deseeded and sliced

1 kaffir lime leaf

1 lemongrass stalk, outer layer removed and the stalk bashed

1 teaspoon peeled and chopped root ginger

1 star anise

olive oil

sea salt and freshly cracked black pepper

For the pork and prawn patties

400g pork mince

100g shelled raw shrimp, finely chopped

50g cleaned squid body, finely chopped

1 tablespoon deseeded and finely chopped fresh red chilli

freshly squeezed juice of 1 lime

2 tablespoons Thai fish sauce

1 tablespoon chopped coriander leaves

To serve

200g rice noodles, cooked according to the packet instructions

toasted sesame oil

150g beansprouts

100g peeled raw prawns

50g shelled broad beans

8 asparagus stalks, trimmed and cut into bite-sized pieces

2 spring onions, thinly sliced

1 fresh red chilli, deseeded and thinly sliced

chopped fresh coriander

Place the chicken stock in a large saucepan and bring to the boil. Add the chilli, kaffir lime leaf, lemongrass, ginger and star anise, and season with salt. Turn off the heat, cover the pan and leave the stock to infuse for 20 minutes. Strain and set aside until required. Discard the flavouring ingredients.

Meanwhile, make the pork and prawn patties. Put all the ingredients in a bowl, season with pepper and mix together. Fry a small amount to taste and check the seasoning – you can always add a little more chilli or salt and pepper, if you like, but the fish sauce will give it lots of flavour. Shape the mixture into 16 golf-ball-sized balls, then flatten. Cover and chill until required.

Just before you are ready to serve, place the rice noodles in a large heatproof bowl. Pour over enough boiling water to cover and leave for 4–5 minutes, or according to the packet instructions, until tender and flexible. Drain well, toss with a little sesame oil and set aside.

Put the infused stock in a saucepan and bring to the boil, then reduce the heat to a simmer.

While the stock is coming to the boil, heat a large well-seasoned sauté or frying pan over a medium heat, then add a thin layer of oil. When it is hot, add the pork patties and fry, turning occasionally, for 6–8 minutes until they are cooked through and browned. Drain the pork patties on kitchen paper and keep hot. Cook in batches, if necessary, to avoid overcrowding the pan.

Divide the rice noodles among 4 large bowls.

Add the beansprouts, prawns, broad beans, asparagus and spring onions to the simmering stock, and continue simmering until the prawns turn pink and are cooked through and the asparagus is tender. Season with salt to taste.

Divide the pork patties among the bowls, then ladle over the vegetables, prawns and hot stock, and sprinkle with the chilli and coriander.

Pigs' Ears with Sauce Gribiche

No doubt about it, home cooks are becoming more and more adventurous, taking on and mastering restaurant techniques. Try this for something a little different for your pre-dinner drink snacks – basically posh pork scratchings! These are a regular on the bar menu at The Scran & Scallie, my Edinburgh gastro pub, and are incredibly easy to make. Even better, you can freeze the ears once they are braised, ready for crisping in the oven when they are required. Don't be shy when it comes to seasoning with salt, as it makes them even more moorish.

SERVES 4

---

6 pigs' ears

2 carrots, peeled and roughly chopped

1 celery stick, chopped

1 white onion, finely chopped

1 bay leaf

1 thyme sprig

4 black peppercorns

olive oil

sea salt and freshly cracked black pepper

For the Sauce Gribiche

4 tablespoons Mayonnaise (page 276)

1 tablespoon finely chopped shallot

2 hard-boiled eggs, shelled and finely
   chopped

1 tablespoon mini capers, drained or
   rinsed as necessary

1 tablespoon finely chopped gherkin

1½ teaspoons finely chopped parsley

½ lemon

Day 1

Preheat the oven to 180°C Fan/200°C/Gas Mark 6 and bring a large saucepan of salted water to the boil. Remove the hairs from the pigs' ears with a blowtorch.

Add the carrots, celery, onion, bay leaf, thyme and peppercorns to the pan of boiling water. Turn the heat to low, add the pigs' ears and place a plate on top to keep them submerged. Partially cover the pan and leave the pigs' ears to simmer for 5–6 hours until they are very tender. Top up the water as necessary.

Meanwhile, line a baking sheet that will fit in your fridge and is large enough to hold the ears in a single layer with greaseproof paper, then set aside. Make sure you have enough height in the fridge for the baking sheet with cans on top.

When the ears are tender, transfer them from the stock to the baking sheet. Leave them to cool completely, then cover them with a layer of clingfilm and place weights on top to press the ears flat – cans of tomatoes and pulses are good to use. Transfer to the fridge and leave overnight. Discard the stock.

Day 2

To make the sauce Gribiche, put the mayonnaise in a bowl and stir in the shallots, eggs, capers, gherkin and parsley. Season with salt and pepper, then taste and stir in a squeeze of lemon juice to taste. Cover and chill until required.

When you're ready to cook, preheat the oven to 200°C Fan/220°C/Gas Mark 7 and line a baking sheet with greaseproof paper.

Cut off any excess cartilage from the ears, then use a sharp knife to cut them into thin strips. Transfer the strips to a bowl, add a splash of olive oil, season lightly with salt and pepper and mix together so the strips are well coated.

Transfer the strips to the baking sheet in a single layer and roast for 35–40 minutes until crisp. When cooked, the ears will stick together like a thin sheet of paper. Remove the baking sheet from the oven and leave the strips to cool and firm up. At this point you can crack them into pieces before serving with the sauce Gribiche. They will stay crisp in an airtight container at room temperature for a couple of days, but are best enjoyed right away.

Pork Cheek Blanquette

Cooking any animal's cheeks, be it pork or beef, always means long, slow braising or stewing, but the flavours you can extract are incredible and the meat is meltingly tender. This is a classic French recipe, traditionally made with veal, that I've changed to pork to make it a little more affordable, but just as tasty. I love to serve this with rice to soak up all the lovely sauce.

--- SERVES 4 ---

12 pork cheeks
200ml dry white wine
6 black peppercorns
2 bay leaves
2 carrots, peeled and thickly chopped
2 garlic cloves, chopped
1 onion, chopped
1 bouquet garni
½ leek, trimmed, chopped and rinsed
2 tablespoons olive oil
100g button mushrooms, trimmed, wiped and quartered
hot boiled long-grain rice, to serve
sea salt and freshly ground black pepper

For the sauce

4 egg yolks
175ml double cream
20g butter
1 tablespoon finely shredded fresh parsley
1 teaspoon wholegrain mustard – I like to use Pommery
finely grated zest and juice of ½ lemon

Leave the pork cheeks to soak in a large bowl of cold water to cover for 1 hour, changing the water every 15 minutes or so.

Drain the cheeks, then transfer them to a large saucepan with cold water to cover, cover the pan and bring to the boil. Drain and discard this first quantity of water. Return the cheeks to the pan with 1.5 litres of fresh cold water and bring to the boil again. Reduce the heat to a simmer and leave the cheeks to simmer for 20 minutes, partially covered and skimming off any froth. Add the wine, peppercorns, bay leaves, carrots, garlic, onion, bouquet garni and leek, and continue simmering for a further 1 hour 40 minutes, or until the meat is tender enough to flake easily.

Meanwhile, heat a well-seasoned sauté or frying pan over a medium-high heat, then add the oil. When it is hot, add the mushrooms with a pinch of salt and sauté for 2–3 minutes until they are tender, browned and have absorbed the liquid they give off. Set aside.

When the pork cheeks are tender, drain them, reserving 1 litre of the poaching liquid and discarding all the flavouring ingredients except the carrots. Set the cheeks and carrots aside and keep hot.

Transfer the reserved liquid to a heavy-based saucepan. Beat the egg yolks and cream for the sauce together. Whisk this mixture into the reserved poaching liquid and stir until it starts to thicken slightly – be careful not to overheat, as the mixture will curdle. Whisk in the butter, then remove the pan from the heat. Add the parsley, mustard and lemon zest and juice, then season with salt and pepper. Reheat the mushrooms, if necessary.

Serve the pork cheeks with the sautéed mushrooms, the reserved carrots, the sauce and hot rice.

Pulled Pork Sandwiches

Tender, juicy pulled pork has certainly made its mark on the British dining scene in the past few years. It wasn't something I had cooked before my son Kasper asked me to make it for his birthday party a few years ago. Since then I've developed a love for pulled pork. The secret to these sandwiches is the lovely juicy pork, but also the underrated red cabbage salad, which cuts through the pork's richness. So simple, but so incredibly tasty.

In summer, when the barbecue is set up and ready to go, I sometimes give the pork its initial browning over the coals for a little extra flavour.

MAKES 4–6 SANDWICHES

1 teaspoon cardamom seeds
1 teaspoon coriander seeds
1 teaspoon fennel seeds
1 teaspoon cracked black peppercorns
3 tablespoons dark brown sugar
2 tablespoons chilli powder
2 tablespoons garlic powder
1 teaspoon ground cumin
1 teaspoon smoked paprika
½ boneless pork shoulder, about 600g,
    rolled and tied
olive oil
4–6 hamburger buns, to serve
sea salt and freshly cracked black pepper

For the barbecue sauce
200g ketchup
50ml white wine vinegar
50g dark brown sugar
2 tablespoons Worcestershire sauce
1 tablespoon clear honey
1 tablespoon molasses
1 tablespoon Dijon mustard
1 tablespoon freshly cracked
    black pepper
1 tablespoon whisky
1 teaspoon finely chopped garlic

For the red cabbage coleslaw
½ red cabbage, cored and thinly sliced
2 carrots, peeled and grated
1 or 2 red onions, thinly sliced
1 teaspoon chopped fresh parsley
100g Mayonnaise (page 276)
sherry vinegar, to taste

Make the barbecue sauce up to 2 days in advance. Mix all the ingredients together in a heavy-based saucepan over a medium heat, stirring for 10–12 minutes until it coats the back of a spoon nicely. Season with salt and pepper, if necessary. It is now ready to use, or can be reheated when mixing with the pork.

You can also make the coleslaw up to a day in advance and keep covered in the fridge. Mix the red cabbage, carrots, onions and parsley together. Stir in the mayonnaise, then season with salt and pepper and splash of sherry vinegar. Cover and chill until required.

Day 1
Heat a well-seasoned sauté or frying pan over a high heat. Add the cardamom, coriander and fennel seeds and black peppercorns, and toast, stirring, for 1–2 minutes until aromatic. Transfer the spices to a mortar and crush until a fine powder forms.

Add the brown sugar, chilli powder, garlic powder, cumin and smoked paprika to the spice powder, and mix together. Set aside.

Pat the pork dry and season all over with salt and pepper. Wipe out the pan with kitchen paper and reheat over a medium-high heat, then add a good splash of oil. When it is hot, add the pork and sear until it is brown all round. Set aside and leave until it is cool enough to handle.

Untie the joint and rub the spice mix into the meat, making sure to cover it all over. Season with salt. Leave to cool completely, then transfer to an ovenproof dish, cover with clingfilm and leave to marinate overnight in the fridge.

Day 2
Preheat the oven to 200°C Fan/220°C/Gas Mark 7. Remove the pork from the fridge about 15 minutes before cooking so it returns to room temperature.

Place the pork shoulder in the oven and roast, covered with kitchen foil, for 20 minutes. Lower the temperature to 140°C Fan/160°C/Gas Mark 3 and leave it to continue roasting for a further 3¼ hours, or until the meat is tender and can easily be pulled apart with forks.

Set aside to rest for 8–10 minutes covered with kitchen foil, and preheat the grill to high.

Meanwhile, reheat the barbecue sauce. Use 2 forks to pull the pork into fine shreds, then mix with the warmed sauce and set aside.

Open the hamburger buns, place them under the grill and toast. Brush them with olive oil, then top with coleslaw and a good serving of the pork.

Smoked Ham Hocks with Hot Pineapple Salsa

The former head chef at our pub, The Scran & Scallie, came up with this dish. We simply serve it with a fried egg and chips and it soon became a favourite with our diners. I have tweaked the recipe slightly for home cooks, but it still has the same great flavours. You can't go wrong with ham hocks – you've got guaranteed flavour if you use any leftovers in a soup or in a stew.

— SERVES 4 —

4 smoked ham hocks, 800–900g each

6 black peppercorns

4 carrots, peeled and chopped

2 garlic cloves, chopped

1 bouquet garni

1 onion, chopped

400g crépinette (pork caul fat), rinsed and cut into 4 equal pieces

olive oil

salt and freshly cracked black pepper

For the hot pineapple salsa

½ ripe pineapple, about 450g, peeled, sliced into 5mm thick rounds, then the core removed and diced

a knob of butter

2 tablespoons olive oil

1 spring onion, finely chopped

1 tablespoon finely chopped chives

2 teaspoons capers, drained and rinsed as necessary

Day 1

Leave the ham hocks to soak in a large bowl of cold water to cover for 1½ hours, changing the water every 15 minutes or so.

Remove the hocks from the water and place in a large heavy-based saucepan or stockpot and cover them with fresh cold water. Bring to the boil, skimming the grey foam from the surface, as necessary. Add the peppercorns, carrots, garlic, bouquet garni and onion. Lower the heat and leave to simmer, partially covered, for 3 hours, or until the meat is tender enough to flake off the bones. Turn off the heat and leave the ham hocks to cool in the liquid.

Day 2

Carefully remove the hocks from the stock and set aside. Strain the stock through a chinois or fine sieve and set aside. Discard the flavouring ingredients.

Preheat the oven to 180°C Fan/200°C/Gas Mark 6.

Meanwhile, carefully remove the skin and bones from the hocks and keep the bone meat from each hock separate. Lay a piece of crépinette on the work surface. Place one portion of ham hock meat on top and shape into an oval mound. Place the bone on top and fold over the crépinette to form a hock-like shape.

Place the hocks in a deep ovenproof dish, pour over enough of the reserved cooking stock to cover the meat and cover the dish with kitchen foil. Place in the oven to braise for 30–35 minutes, basting regularly, until a metal skewer inserted into the centre comes out hot and the caul fat starts to seal. Season with salt and pepper, but remember the stock might have been salty.

Meanwhile, to make the hot pineapple salsa, pat the pineapple pieces dry with kitchen paper. Heat a well-seasoned sauté pan over a medium heat, then melt the butter with the oil. When it is sizzling, add the pineapple and sauté for 40–50 seconds, then add the spring onions, chives and capers and continue sautéing for a couple of minutes until lightly coloured and softened.

To serve, reheat the pineapple salsa, if necessary, and serve spooned over the hocks.

Ham and Leek Pie

Whenever I'm writing a cookbook I start to become a little nostalgic and remember childhood favourites. This dish certainly reminds me of my those days, and I now totally understand why my mother loved cooking this pie. Not only is it delicious, but it's a great dish to get ready in the morning for popping in the oven later, allowing you to get on with the day.

SERVES 4

---

olive oil

2 large leeks, trimmed, sliced and rinsed

1 onion, chopped

2 garlic cloves, finely chopped

2 tablespoons plain flour, plus extra for rolling out the pastry

300ml Chicken Stock (page 279)

400g cooked ham, finely diced

100ml crème fraîche

1 teaspoon wholegrain mustard – I like to use Pommery

375g puff pastry, thawed if frozen

1 egg yolk, beaten

sea salt and freshly cracked black pepper

Heat a well-seasoned sauté or frying pan over a medium heat, then add the oil. When it is hot, add the leek and onion and sauté for 2 minutes. Add the garlic and continue sautéing until the leeks and onion are softened, but not coloured. Season with salt and pepper.

Sprinkle over the flour and stir for 1–2 minutes to cook out the raw flour, then slowly stir in the chicken stock. Add the ham, crème fraîche and mustard, and stir together. Adjust the seasoning with salt and pepper, if necessary. Set aside.

Roll out the pastry on a lightly floured surface with a lightly floured rolling pin until it is about 2cm thick. Cut a strip of pastry the same width as the rim of a 2-litre pie dish. Lightly brush the edge of the dish with a little of the beaten egg yolk and fix the strip around it. Spoon the filling into the pie dish.

Brush the top of the pastry strip with egg yolk, then lay over the remaining pastry and press down lightly and crimp the edge. Cut off the excess pastry to trim the edge. Use a small knife to cut a steam hole in the centre, then insert a foil funnel to release the steam while baking. Leave the pie to chill for at least 20 minutes before baking.

Meanwhile, preheat the oven to 200°C Fan/220°C/Gas Mark 7.

When you're ready to bake the pie, brush the surface with egg yolk. Place the pie on a baking sheet and bake for 35–45 minutes, or until the filling is piping hot and the pastry is well risen and golden brown. Set aside to rest for 5 minutes before serving.

Whole Suckling Pig

Before you begin you need to make sure the suckling pig is going to fit into your oven. As you'll probably need to pre-order the pig, you can discuss what size you can handle with your butcher. At home, I try to cook this dish once a year for a special occasion. The joy of seeing kids (and adults) picking away is fantastic. Make sure you don't lose any of the fantastic cooking juices and don't forget to try the trotters! My favourite!

— SERVES 6–8 —

7kg free-range and high-welfare whole suckling pig, cleaned
3 apples, cored and chopped
2 celery sticks, chopped
2 whole garlic heads, separated into cloves and chopped
2 onions, chopped
1 lemon, sliced
1 bunch fresh thyme
a handful rosemary sprigs
1 tablespoon cracked black peppercorns
1 teaspoon green cardamom pods, cracked
1 teaspoon fennel seeds
olive oil
sea salt and freshly cracked black pepper

Preheat the oven to 200°C Fan/220°C/Gas Mark 7.

Using a small, sharp knife, carefully score the skin all over with slashes about 1cm deep and roughly 2cm apart, taking care not to cut into the flesh. Set aside.

Mix together the apples, celery, garlic, onions, lemon, thyme, rosemary, peppercorns, cardamom pods and fennel seeds with a good splash of olive oil. Season with salt, then carefully spoon the mixture into the pig's stomach. Pack it tightly to ensure the stuffing stays in place. Truss the belly with a trussing needle or you can use metal skewers. Rub olive oil all over and give the pig a good sprinkling of salt and pepper – it's nice to wrap the ears and tail with kitchen foil to stop them burning. Place the pig in a large roasting tray with a smaller tray under it for support.

Wrap 2 layers of kitchen foil over the pig and the tray, scrunching it tightly. Transfer the pig to the oven and roast for 20–25 minutes. Lower the oven temperature to 160°C Fan/180°C/Gas Mark 4, remove the foil covering (but leave it on the ears and tail) and continue roasting for a further 3 hours, basting frequently, or until the pig is tender and the juices run clear when you pierce a thigh with a skewer. If the skin is browning too much, cover it with foil for the last half hour or so.

Remove the pig from the oven and set aside to rest for 20 minutes covered with kitchen foil.

Transfer the stuffing mixture to a mixing bowl, remove the cardamom pods and season with salt and pepper.

Carefully portion the pig, making sure you serve everyone with a share of the lovely crispy skin and a spoonful of the stuffing.

Slow-roast Shoulder of Lamb with French Bean Salad

When I was a young chef in the South of France, I worked with a guy called Laurent, from Aix-en-Provence. We used to visit his parents' house and they would cook a slow-roasted shoulder of lamb over a wood fire. It was sensational! This recipe is totally inspired by that dish and it works well in an oven, too. The meat should flake off the bone when cooked.

SERVES 6

1 lamb shoulder, 2.5–3kg
1 tablespoon fennel seeds
1 teaspoon ground cumin
1 teaspoon smoked paprika
olive oil
1 tablespoon thyme leaves
1 tablespoon rosemary needles
sea salt and freshly cracked black pepper

For the French bean salad
300g French beans, trimmed
60g toasted hazelnuts, chopped
5 garlic cloves, finely chopped
2 shallots, very finely chopped
hazelnut oil

Place the lamb on a chopping board and use a small knife to make a few slits all over. Use a large pestle and mortar to grind the fennel seeds, ground cumin and paprika with a good splash of olive oil and salt and pepper to crush the seeds. Add the thyme and rosemary leaves and mix together.

Using your hands, massage the spice and herb rub on to the shoulder and especially into the little slits. Cover the lamb with clingfilm and set aside for at least 20 minutes, or up to 3 hours.

Meanwhile, preheat the oven to 220°C Fan/240°C/Gas Mark 9.

Place the shoulder in a heavy-based roasting tray and roast for 30 minutes so it seals well and takes on some colour. Now cover the lamb with kitchen foil and turn the oven temperature down to 170°C Fan/190°C/Gas Mark 5 and continue roasting for a further 4 hours, or until the meat is tender enough to flake from the bone.

Remove the lamb from the oven and set aside to rest for about 15 minutes covered with kitchen foil. Discard the fatty cooking juices in the tray.

While the lamb is resting, bring a large saucepan of salted water to the boil and place a bowl of iced water in the sink. Add the beans to the boiling water and boil for 4 minutes, or until tender. Drain them and immediately transfer them to the iced water to stop the cooking.

Drain the beans again, then transfer to a large bowl. Add the hazelnuts, garlic, shallots, a good splash of hazelnut oil and salt, and toss together. Serve the lamb with the French bean salad alongside.

Sautéed Lamb Sweetbreads and Baby Artichokes on Sourdough Toast

I'm a great lover of the forgotten cuts. For many people the thought of eating offal is too much, but sweetbreads are just fantastic. I really enjoy serving this dish to people when I'm cooking at home, as nine times out of ten they would never order it on a menu or cook it themselves. The trick is to get the sweetbreads nice and caramelised and guests will love them.

SERVES 4

300g lamb sweetbreads, trimmed

2 baby artichokes, in season

1 lemon

100g podded broad beans

2 teaspoons mixed chopped garlic and parsley

4 thick slices of sourdough bread

olive oil

marjoram leaves, to garnish

sea salt and freshly cracked black pepper

Place the sweetbreads into a bowl of cold water and leave them submerged for 45 minutes, changing the water every 15 minutes, or until the water isn't pink.

If you're using the baby artichokes, prepare them while the sweetbreads are soaking. Squeeze the juice from half the lemon into another bowl of cold water and set aside. Cut off the top third of the artichoke, then peel off the green outer leaves until you get down to the pale yellow leaves, rubbing the surface with the other half of the lemon to prevent browning. If there are any thick leaf bases left, cut them off, then trim the stalk. Quarter the artichoke lengthways and drop the pieces in the lemon water. Because this is a baby artichoke, there shouldn't be any of the inedible hairy choke, but if you see any of the pale yellow 'hairs' use a teaspoon to scoop out and discard. Repeat with the remaining artichoke.

Before the sweetbreads finish soaking, preheat the grill to high. Bring a small saucepan of salted water to the boil and place a bowl of iced water in the sink. When the water is boiling, add the broad beans and blanch for 2 minutes, or until just tender. Drain well and immediately transfer to the iced water to stop the cooking. Drain again and set aside.

Remove the sweetbreads from the water when it is clear and pat dry with a kitchen towel. Use a small sharp knife to remove any sinew, then set aside.

Heat a small well-seasoned sauté or frying pan over a high heat, then add a splash of oil. When it is hot, season the sweetbreads with salt and pepper, add them to the pan and fry on one side for 3 minutes, or until lightly coloured.

Meanwhile, toast the bread under the hot grill until it is golden brown on both sides. Drain the artichoke pieces well, pat dry and set aside.

Gently turn the sweetbreads over, add the artichoke pieces to the pan and sauté for 2–3 minutes until the artichokes are softened. Add the broad beans, garlic and parsley and continue sautéing until the beans are hot and the sweetbreads are lightly coloured. Adjust the seasoning with salt and pepper, if necessary.

To serve, drizzle the hot toasts with olive oil, then divide the sweetbread mixture among the pieces of toast and sprinkle with marjoram leaves.

Haggis, Pickled Neep and Tatties

Haggis, neeps and tatties is a Scottish classic and traditionally always eaten on Burns Night. Neeps are better knows as swedes and tatties as potatoes outside Scotland. For this recipe I've tried to lighten it up a little as it can be quite filling. The pickled neeps are great fun and could easily be used in a salad.

— SERVES 4 —

vegetable oil
50g smoked lardons
4 black peppercorns
2 carrots, peeled and chopped
1 onion, chopped
2 garlic cloves, chopped
1 celery stick, chopped
200ml full-bodied red wine
100ml brandy
100ml Madeira
100ml port
400ml Beef Stock (page 278), plus extra
    as needed
1 bouquet garni
400g pork belly skin, cut into equal 4
    pieces
1 haggis, about 500g
butter, softened for brushing the foil
flat-leaf parsley leaves, to garnish
sea salt and freshly cracked black pepper

For the pickled neep

500ml water
150ml white wine vinegar
150g caster sugar
5 black peppercorns
1 bay leaf
1 or 2 garlic cloves, to taste, peeled and
    crushed
½ swede, peeled and cut into
    matchsticks

For the tatties

1kg flour potatoes, such as Maris Piper,
    peeled and quartered
60g unsalted butter
100ml whole milk
freshly ground white pepper

Preheat the oven to 160°C Fan/180°C/Gas Mark 4.

Heat a flameproof casserole over a medium-high heat, then add a splash of oil. When it is hot, add the lardons and sauté until they render their fat and are coloured all over. Add the peppercorns, carrots, onion, garlic and celery, and sauté for a further 2–3 minutes until the vegetables are beginning to colour and soften.

Add the red wine, brandy, Madeira and port, stirring to deglaze the pan, and boil until the liquid almost evaporates. Add the beef stock and bouquet garni and return to the boil. Season with salt and pepper.

Add the pork skin to the boiling stock, cover the casserole and place in the oven for about 3 hours until the skin is flaky and has a braised colour.

Meanwhile, make the pickled neep. Place the water, vinegar, sugar, peppercorns, bay leaf and garlic in a heavy-based saucepan over a high heat, stirring to dissolve the sugar, then bring to the boil. Taste – it should have a sweet/sour flavour, so add more sugar or vinegar, if necessary. Add the neep and season with salt, then cover the pan, remove it from the heat and leave the neep to soften in the liquid for 1–2 hours.

To make the tatties, place the potato pieces in a saucepan of salted water. Bring to the boil, then boil for 15 minutes, or until the potatoes are very tender. Drain well, then return them to the pan. Melt the butter with the milk in a small saucepan. Use a potato masher to crush the potatoes, then slowly add the butter and continue mashing until they are smooth. Season with salt and white pepper and set aside until required.

Also, while the neep is pickling, cook the haggis according to the packet instructions.

Remove the haggis from the casing and shape into 4 equal portions. Cover with clingfilm and set aside until required.

Continued on page 58

When the pork skin is tender, carefully strain the cooking liquid and set the skin aside until it is cool enough to handle, then remove the excess fat. Discard the flavouring ingredients, but reserve the liquid.

Cut out 4 sheets of kitchen foil, each about 45 x 30cm. Place one sheet of foil on the work surface and lightly butter it. Add a piece of pork skin, then top with one of the haggis sausages. Tightly roll the foil around the haggis, twisting the ends to create a boudin, or thick sausage shape, each about 10cm long. Repeat to make 3 more haggis rolls. At this point you can transfer the haggis rolls to the fridge for up to 2 days or continue with the recipe.

To serve, steam the haggis rolls for 15–20 minutes until they are hot in the middle. Test by inserting a metal skewer and it should feel hot if you press it to your lip.

Meanwhile, transfer the reserved pork stock to saucepan and boil until it reduces by half. Adjust the salt and pepper, if necessary. Reheat the tatties.

Remove the haggis from the steamer and trim the edges, then remove the foil and divide among your serving plates. Drain the pickled neep and pat dry.

Glaze the haggis with the reduced stock and divide the remaining stock among your serving plates, or serve in a jug on the side. Serve the hot haggis with the pickled neep and tatties, garnished with parsley leaves.

Herb-crusted Rack of Lamb with Ratatouille

Rack of lamb is the most expensive cut on the lamb but is certainly worth it if you're looking to treat yourself. The herb breadcrumbs are a great way of bringing even more flavours to the dish but could also be used with other meats or even fish. The combination of lamb and ratatouille is perfect.

SERVES 4

---

2 x 4-bone racks of lamb, well trimmed
with all the fat removed
olive oil
50g Dijon mustard
sea salt and freshly cracked black pepper

For the ratatouille
2 red peppers
1 yellow pepper
olive oil
1 onion, chopped
2 garlic cloves, coarsely chopped
1 tablespoon thyme leaves
2 courgettes, cut into 2.5cm dice
1 tablespoon ground cumin
2 aubergines, cut into 2.5cm dice
10 cherry tomatoes, cut in half
basil leaves, to garnish

For the herbed breadcrumbs
10g parsley leaves
7g basil leaves
5g chervil leaves
5g tarragon leaves
1 garlic clove, chopped
100g fine dried breadcrumbs

First make the ratatouille up to 4–5 hours before you plan to serve. If you have a gas stove, light the gas and carefully place the red and yellow peppers on top of the burner so the flames actually char the skins, using a roasting fork or tongs to turn them so they char all over. If you don't have a gas hob, use a blow torch. Once the peppers are charred, wrap them individually in clingfilm and set aside for 10 minutes – this makes the peppers sweat so you can remove the skins easily.

Remove the clingfilm and place the peppers into a sieve or colander in the sink and rinse off the skins with cold running water. The sieve catches all the bits and stops your sink from becoming blocked. Remove the seeds and place the peppers on kitchen towel to dry, then cut them into 2.5cm pieces like the other vegetables and set aside.

Heat a large well-seasoned sauté or frying pan over a medium heat, then add a good splash of olive oil. When the oil is hot, add the onion to the large pan and sauté for 2–3 minutes until it is beginning to soften. Add the garlic and thyme and continue sautéing until the onion is softened but not coloured.

Meanwhile, heat another pan over a medium-high heat then add a splash of oil. When it is hot, add the courgettes and sauté until they are softened, then sprinkle with half the ground cumin and season with salt. Tip out of the pan and set aside.

Return the pan to medium-high heat and heat another good splash of oil. Add the aubergine, season with the remaining cumin and a pinch of salt and sauté for 5 minutes, or until they are softened, then add to the courgette. You'll probably have to add more oil while the aubergine cooks because it will absorb quite a bit.

Add the courgette, aubergine and red peppers to the onions, then stir everything together for 2–3 minutes to blend the flavours. Add the cherry tomatoes and bring to the boil, stirring, then turn off the heat and set aside until required if you're not serving immediately.

Continued on page 61

To make the herbed breadcrumbs, place all the ingredients in a food processor and pulse until the mixture becomes bright green. Set aside.

When you're ready to cook the lamb, preheat the oven to 200°C Fan/220°C/Gas Mark 7 and spread out the herbed breadcrumbs in a shallow tray or another flat container.

Heat a large well-seasoned, ovenproof sauté or frying pan over a medium-high heat, then add a splash of oil. Season the racks all over with salt and pepper, then add them to the pan and fry until nice and brown. Transfer the pan to the oven and roast the racks for 3 minutes, then turn over and roast for a further 3–4 minutes for rare meat.

Remove the pan from the oven and use a pastry brush to brush the side of each rack where the fat was with mustard, then roll them in the herbed breadcrumbs, gently patting the crumbs in place. Set aside to rest, covered with kitchen foil, for 5 minutes while reheating the ratatouille, if necessary, then stir in the basil into the ratatouille.

To serve, cut the racks into individual cutlets and serve on a bed of ratatouille.

Braised Lamb Shanks with Lemon Confit

Lamb shanks are one of the great comfort foods. The meat has incredible flavour. The key is to really slow cook the lamb shanks so the meat becomes meltingly tender and falls off the bone. If you don't have a casserole large enough for this recipe, use a heavy-based roasting tray tightly covered with kitchen foil. Scrunch the edges well, so none of the liquid escapes.

— SERVES 4 —

4 lamb shanks
olive oil
2 carrots, peeled and chopped
2 celery sticks, chopped
1 fennel head, chopped
1 onion, chopped
1 garlic head, separated into cloves,
    peeled and lightly crushed
2 tablespoons tomato purée
freshly grated zest of 1 lemon
300ml dry white wine
1 bouquet garni
2 litres Lamb Stock (page 278)
Lemon Confit (page 277), to garnish
thyme leaves, to garnish
sea salt and freshly cracked black pepper

Preheat the oven to 180°C Fan/200°C/Gas Mark 6.

While the oven is heating, season the lamb shanks with salt and pepper. Heat a well-seasoned sauté or frying pan over a medium-high heat, then add a thin layer of olive oil. When it is hot, add the lamb shanks and brown them really well all over, then remove and set aside. You will have to do this in batches.

Heat a little more oil in a flameproof casserole large enough to hold all the shanks. Add the carrots, celery, fennel and onion, and sauté for 3–4 minutes until they are softened. Add the garlic cloves, tomato purée and lemon zest, and sauté for a further 1–2 minutes to cook out the raw flavour of the tomato purée. Season with salt and pepper.

Add the white wine, stirring to deglaze the pan, and boil until it evaporates. Add the lamb shanks and bouquet garni, pour over the stock and season with salt and pepper. Cover the casserole and bring the stock to the boil on the hob. Transfer the casserole to the oven and leave the shanks to braise for 2½ hours, or until the meat is tender enough to flake from the bones.

Remove the shanks from the casserole and set aside.

Strain the cooking juices through a chinois or fine sieve into a saucepan, then return the shanks to the casserole, cover and set aside. Bring the juices to the boil and leave until they are reduced by half. Adjust the seasoning if necessary.

Return the juices to the casserole, then baste the shanks all over and reheat if necessary. Serve the shanks sprinkled with lemon confit and thyme leaves.

Barnsley Chops with a Spicy Olive Relish

Of course we all love the tenderness of lamb loin, but ask any butcher or chef which their favourite cut is and I'm sure a lot will say Barnsley chop. It is cut across the saddle so you get a double helping of loin, but also some lovely fillet and around a generous amount of fat that keeps it juicy when cooking. The spicy relish works really well with the lamb, but keep any leftovers in an airtight container in the fridge to jazz up other lamb dishes or some chicken, or even a piece of salmon.

These chops are also good barbecued. If you want to do that, light the coals until they are grey and glowing and grease the grill rack. Cook the chops for 2–3 minutes, then turn them over and move them to a slightly cooler part of the grill and cook for a further 2–3 minutes, depending on size, for medium-rare meat. Set aside and leave to rest for 5 minutes covered with kitchen foil.

SERVES 4

4 Barnsley chops, 340g each – ask your butcher to prepare these for you
olive oil
1 garlic head, separated into cloves
1 rosemary sprig, plus extra to garnish
1 thyme sprig, plus extra to garnish
2 teaspoons cumin powder
mixed green salad, to serve (optional)
sea salt and freshly cracked black pepper

For the olive relish
2 garlic cloves
2 fresh red chillies, deseeded and chopped
1 green chilli, deseeded and chopped
10g coriander leaves
10g mint leaves
10g parsley leaves
100g mixed green and black olives, drained if necessary, rinsed and stoned
1 tablespoon sherry vinegar
1 lemon, halved
100ml extra virgin olive oil

First make the olive relish, which will keep for up to 2 days in a covered container in the fridge. Halve and remove the germ from each garlic clove, then crush them well using a large pestle and mortar. Add the red and green chillies and crush again, followed by all the herbs, crushing, grinding and pounding until the ingredients are broken down. Add the olives and continue pounding together.

Add the sherry vinegar, squeeze in lemon juice to taste and slowly pour the olive oil as you continue grinding everything together, so a thick paste forms. Season with salt and pepper and set aside.

Begin marinating the chops at least 2 hours before you plan to cook them. Place them in a dish with a good covering of oil, then add the garlic cloves, rosemary and thyme. Sprinkle with the cumin, then cover with clingfilm and place in the fridge for 1½–2 hours.

Remove the chops from the fridge 30 minutes before you plan to cook, so they return to room temperature.

You could cook these on a barbecue, as per the introduction. Alternatively, heat a large well-seasoned cast-iron, ridged griddle over a high heat. Cook the chops for 2 minutes to sear them and cook the fat, then lower the temperature under the griddle pan to medium and cook for a further 2 minutes. Turn them over and cook for a further 3 minutes, which should give you pink and juicy meat. Set aside to rest for 5 minutes covered with kitchen foil.

Serve, garnished with fresh rosemary and thyme, with the relish on the side and a green salad, if you like. Any juices that accumulate during the resting period are delicious spooned over.

Braised Lamb Neck with Pea and Lettuce Ragoût

Lamb necks are unbelievably under-valued, but such great value for money. If you've not cooked them before I think you'll be surprised at how much meat you get off a neck. Don't be shy to season generously with salt and pepper so the neck takes on a good flavour.

If you like, fire up the barbecue and brown the meat on that rather than the sauté pan as mentioned below.

— SERVES 4 —

1 large whole lamb neck, about 1.65kg, cut in half, ask a butcher to do this

olive oil

2 carrots, peeled and chopped

2 tomatoes, chopped

1 fennel head, trimmed and chopped

1 garlic head, separated into cloves and peeled

1 onion, chopped

1 red pepper, cored, deseeded and chopped

6 green cardamom pods, bruised

1 teaspoon fennel seeds

1 tablespoon curry powder

1 tablespoon tomato purée

300ml dry white wine

2 litres Lamb Stock (page 278)

1 bouquet garni

ground cumin, to taste

sea salt and freshly cracked black pepper

For the pea and lettuce ragoût

2 carrots, peeled and diced

70g smoked lardons

450g shelled peas, use frozen if you like

1 baby gem lettuce, chopped

Preheat the oven to 180°C Fan/200°C/Gas Mark 6.

Pat the lamb neck dry. Heat a well-seasoned large sauté or frying pan over a medium-high heat, then add a splash of olive oil. When it is hot, add the neck pieces and leave them to colour on all sides, then set aside.

Heat a large flameproof casserole over a medium-high heat, then add a splash of oil. When it is hot, add the carrots, tomatoes, fennel, garlic cloves, onion, red pepper, cardamom pods, fennel seeds and curry powder with a pinch of salt, and sauté until the vegetables are beginning to soften. Add the tomato purée and stir for another minute to cook out the raw flavour.

Add the white wine, stirring to deglaze the pan, and boil until it evaporates. Add the lamb stock and bouquet garni, followed by the lamb neck. Season with salt and pepper. Cover the casserole and bring the stock to the boil. Transfer the casserole to the oven and leave the lamb to braise for 3–3½ hours until the meat is tender enough to flake from the bone.

Meanwhile, bring a small saucepan of salted water to the boil and put a bowl of iced water in the sink. Add the carrots for the ragoût to the boiling water and blanch until they are just tender, then drain well. Immediately add them to the iced water. When they are cool, drain them well and set aside.

About 8 minutes before you plan to serve, make the ragoût. Heat a well-seasoned sauté or frying pan over a medium-high heat, then add a splash of oil. When it is hot, add the lardons and sauté until they render their fat and are coloured all over. Set the pan aside to finish the ragoût after the lamb finishes cooking.

When the neck is tender, remove it from the casserole and season with salt and pepper and a pinch of cumin. Cover with kitchen foil and set aside.

Strain the lamb cooking juices through a chinois or fine sieve into a saucepan and boil until reduced by half. Adjust the seasoning with salt and pepper, if necessary.

To finish the ragout, add the peas, blanched carrots, 150ml of the reduced cooking juices to the pan with the lardons. and leave to bubble until the peas are tender. Stir in the lettuce and continue simmering until it wilts. Adjust the seasoning, if necessary.

Transfer the ragoût to a serving platter, add the braised lamb necks and serve the remaining cooking juices on the side.

Stuffed Saddle of Hogget

Hogget is sheep meat from an animal between one and two years old, and is often overlooked by many cooks. It is simply a delicious mix of lamb and mutton. For this recipe, get your butcher to help with the butchery, and once the joint's cooked, remember to give the meat a good rest in a warm place before slicing it. Any juices that accumulate while it's resting shouldn't be wasted and are excellent spooned over the slices.

SERVES 4

1 bone-in saddle of lamb, about 1.25kg, trimmed of fat

300g spinach, thick central stalks removed

olive oil

2 tablespoons coarsely chopped lamb's kidney

1 tablespoon coarsely chopped black olives

1 tablespoon chopped shallot

200g crépinette (pork caul fat), rinsed

2 teaspoons finely chopped rosemary

sea salt and freshly cracked black pepper

When you order the saddle, ask the butcher to remove the bone but keep the belly attached. Ask him or her to pull off the membrane and baton out the belly very carefully, not breaking the fat. You should end up with about 700g boneless meat. Be sure to ask for the kidneys to be coarsely chopped for using in the stuffing.

First cook the spinach. Rinse the spinach well, then shake it dry. Add it to a heavy-based saucepan over a medium heat with just the water clinging to the leaves and a pinch of salt, then stir until it wilts and is tender. Tip the spinach into a colander to drain, then squeeze out any remaining liquid. Set aside.

Heat a large well-seasoned sauté or frying pan over a medium-high heat, then add a splash of oil. When it's hot, add the kidney, season with salt and pepper and quickly sauté until it is cooked through. Add the spinach, black olives and shallot, and stir together. Adjust the seasoning with salt and pepper, if necessary, then set aside to cool completely.

Meanwhile, preheat the oven to 200°C Fan/220°C/Gas Mark 7.

Spread out the crépinette on a work surface. Place the lamb on top, skin side down. Season the flesh with the rosemary and salt and pepper. Place the spinach stuffing on top of the battened-out belly, then lift the belly flap up and over the loin. Wrap the loin in the crepinette, then tie it in place with kitchen string. Season the lamb all over with salt and pepper.

Heat a large well-seasoned, ovenproof sauté or frying pan over a medium-high heat, then add a splash of oil. Add the rolled loin and brown all over. Transfer the pan to the oven and roast for 8 minutes per 100g. The meat is cooked through when you insert a metal skewer through the centre and it feels hot when you then put it on your lips.

Transfer the lamb from the oven to a platter with a rim and set aside to rest for 10 minutes covered with kitchen foil. The juices on the plater are quite delicious, but you need to skin the fat off the surface before spooning them over the meat when serving.

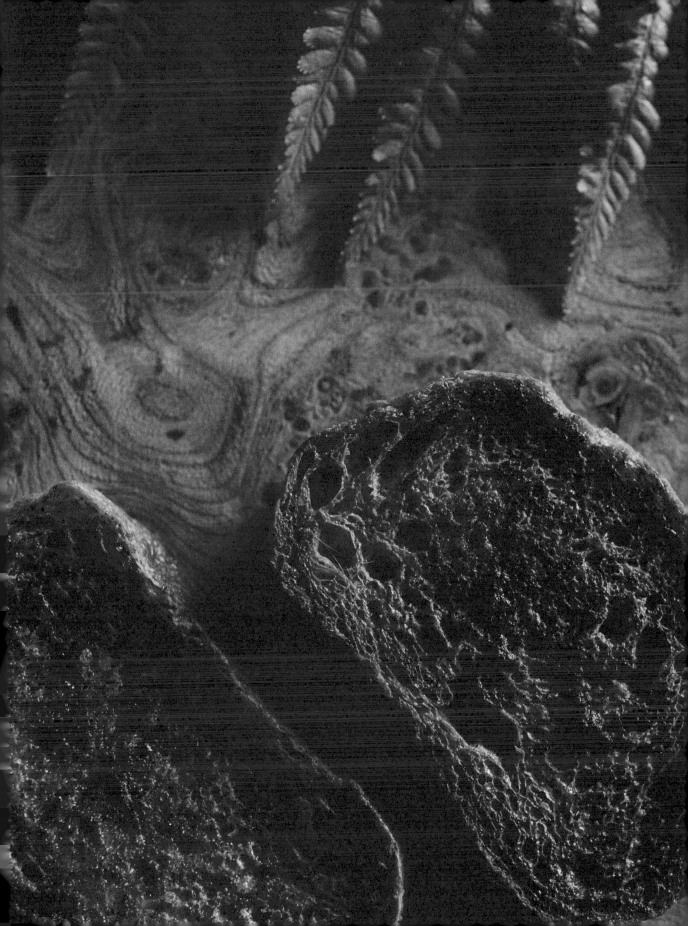

Venison

Roast Rack of Venison with a Blueberry and Juniper Crust

Venison loin is a lean meat, low in fat and full of flavour, and becoming more and more widely available. The gamy flavour works fantastically well with autumn and winter fruit, such as apples, cranberries, and with blueberries and bramble berries, which I combine in the mixed berry compôte. I also highlight this great flavour combination by using blueberries in the juniper-flavoured crust. The drying of the blueberry and juniper crust needs a bit of imagination to dry it if your oven does not have such a low setting.

SERVES 4

4 x 5-rib racks of roe deer, 250g each
vegetable oil
50g butter
2 garlic cloves, finely chopped
1 tablespoon chopped fresh rosemary and thyme leaves
250g kale, well rinsed with any coarse stalks removed
2 tablespoons Dijon mustard
sea salt and freshly cracked black pepper

For the blueberry and juniper crust
300g fresh or frozen blueberries (if you can get wild, even better)
20 juniper berries

For the mixed berry compôte
150g bramble berries or blackberries
150g blueberries
60g caster sugar
½ cinnamon stick
½ lemon

Preheat your oven to it's lowest setting, such as 90°C Fan/110°C/Gas Mark ¼. If your oven doesn't have such a low setting, however, you can use any warm place, such as an airing cupboard. Line a shallow baking tray with a sheet of greaseproof paper and set aside.

Place the blueberries in a blender or food processor and blend until smooth, then pass through a chinois or fine sieve. Spread the blueberry purée evenly to a thickness of about 1cm all over the greaseproof paper, the transfer to the oven and leave to dry for 3–4 hours, checking occasionally that it doesn't burn, but also isn't completely dry.

Meanwhile, heat a small well-seasoned sauté or frying pan over a medium-high heat and gently toast the juniper berries for 1–2 minutes until they start to become aromatic. Use a large pestle and mortar to grind the berries.

When the blueberry purée is dry, break it into pieces and add it to the ground juniper berries and grind together. (Alternatively, you can use a small food processor.) Transfer to an air-tight container and set aside until required.

The berry compôte can be made up to 3 days in advance and chilled until required. Put the bramble berries, blueberries, 40g of the sugar and the cinnamon stick in a heavy-based saucepan over a medium-high heat and stir until the blueberries start to burst, both berries release their juice and all the sugar dissolves. Keep a careful eye on the mixture as the sugar dissolves. Bring to the boil, then reduce the heat and simmer for 10–15 minutes, stirring occasionally, until soft. Taste and add as much of the remaining 20g sugar as you like. Remove the compôte from the heat and leave to cool completely. Adjust the flavour with freshly squeezed lemon juice as you like, and store in the fridge until ready to use.

Continued on page 74

When you're ready to cook, preheat the oven to 200°C Fan/220°C/Gas Mark 7 and bring a large saucepan of salted water to the boil. Remove the compôte from the fridge so it comes to room temperature.

Season the venison racks well with salt and rub in the black pepper. Heat a large well-seasoned sauté or frying pan over a medium-high heat, then add a splash of oil. Place as many racks as will fit in the pan, fat side down, and leave for 2–3 minutes to colour well. As they are browned, transfer them to a heavy-based roasting tray, and continue with the remaining racks.

Add 30g of the butter to the pan. When it starts foaming, pour it over the racks in the roasting tray and baste the meat well, then add the garlic cloves, rosemary and thyme.

Transfer the tray to the oven and leave the racks to roast for 4–5 minutes, which should produce pink meat. Set aside and leave to rest for 5 minutes, covered with kitchen foil, on a plate with a rim to catch all the juices.

Meanwhile, add the kale to the boiling water and boil for 40–50 seconds until tender. Drain well and season with salt and pepper, then add the remaining 20g butter.

When the meat has rested, use a pastry brush to brush the surface with the Dijon mustard, then roll in the blueberry and juniper crust, pressing it on. Cut the rack into ribs, spoon any of the accumulated cooking juices alongside and serve with the kale and mixed berry compôte.

Venison Burgers with Celeriac Soup and Fried Quail's Eggs

I love how this dish comes together; it makes me smile as it gets people's attention as they find it amusing to serve a burger in a soup. Celeriac soup is one of the highlights of winter cooking for me, it is so rich and velvety but so full of flavours, and I also find it a lovely white colour when blended. Don't forget to add the juice of lemon when cooking as the acidity will really help.

SERVES 4

15g butter

vegetable oil

½ onion, finely chopped

½ garlic clove, crushed

2 teaspoons herbes de Provence

240g haunch of venison shoulder, minced

100g pork belly fat, minced

1 free-range egg, beaten

20g fresh breadcrumbs

2 teaspoons Dijon mustard

4 quail's eggs

sea salt and freshly cracked white pepper

For the celeriac soup

1 whole celeriac

15g butter

olive oil

1 onion, sliced

500ml Chicken Stock (page 279)

500ml milk

freshly squeezed juice of ½ lemon

To garnish

1 green apple

30g cooked chestnuts, sliced

1 tablespoon chopped chives

freshly cracked black pepper

extra virgin olive oil

First make the celeriac soup, which will keep for 2–3 days in a covered container in the fridge. Peel the celeriac, then cut it into 2.5cm cubes and set aside.

Heat a well-seasoned saucepan over a high heat, then melt the butter with a splash of oil. When the butter is foaming, add the onion and a pinch of salt and sauté for 2–3 minutes until the onion is softened, but not coloured.

Add the celeriac, cover with a piece of greaseproof paper, cover the pan with a lid and leave it to sweat for 2–3 minutes until it softens, but doesn't colour. Add the chicken stock, milk and lemon juice. Bring to the boil, skimming the surface, then reduce the heat and simmer, uncovered, for about 20 minutes until the celeriac is very tender. Do not worry if the milk curdles because you are going to blend the soup and it will be fine.

Transfer to a blender or food processor and mix until smooth. Adjust the seasoning with salt and white pepper, then set aside or chill until required.

To make the venison burgers, heat a well-seasoned sauté or frying pan over a medium-high heat, then melt the butter with a splash of oil. When the butter foams, add the onion, garlic and a pinch of salt, and sauté for 1–2 minutes until the onion is softened, but not coloured. Add the dried herbs and continue sautéing for a further minute, then set aside to cool completely.

Place the venison and pork belly in to a bowl and mix well together. Add the cool onion mix, egg, breadcrumbs and mustard, and season well with salt and pepper, mixing to incorporate all the ingredients. Fry a small amount in a well-seasoned pan to taste and adjust the salt and pepper, if necessary.

Once you are happy with the seasoning, wet your hands lightly and shape the mix into 4 equal-sized patties.

Continued on page 77

Heat a large well-seasoned sauté or frying pan over a medium heat, then add a splash of oil. When it is hot, add the venison patties and cook for 4–5 minutes, turning them once and making sure they are not over-cooked. Set them aside and keep hot.

Wipe out the pan, then heat a thin layer of oil. One by one, crack the quail's eggs into the pan and fry until they are done as you like them. Transfer to a piece of kitchen paper to drain.

Meanwhile, reheat the soup without boiling, and adjust the seasoning, if necessary. Halve, core and cut the apple into 5mm cubes.

To serve, place a burger in the centre of 4 bowls and top each with a fried egg. Gently ladle the soup around the burgers and garnish with the apple, chestnuts, chives and black pepper. Drizzle with olive oil and serve.

Venison Tartare with Hazelnut Mayonnaise

I prepared this dish on *Saturday Kitchen* once, and the feedback was so good I decided to include it in this book. It is well known that the French have been making beef tartare forever, but in this version I'm still using a raw fillet, albeit venison, and I've added diced raw vegetables and apple and included hazelnut-flavoured mayonnaise to bind everything together for the authentic texture with originality. This dish makes a great starter for a dinner party, as all the ingredients can be prepared in advance so you only have to mix them together just before plating and serving.

SERVES 4

400g roe deer fillet

2 tablespoons peeled and finely chopped apple

2 tablespoons peeled and finely chopped carrot

2 tablespoons peeled and finely chopped celeriac

2 tablespoons finely chopped chives

2 tablespoons roughly chopped hazelnuts

1 teaspoon finely chopped shallots

1 teaspoon sherry vinegar

4 quail's eggs

sea salt and freshly cracked black pepper

For the hazelnut mayonnaise

1 free-range egg yolk

1 teaspoon Dijon mustard

1 teaspoon sherry vinegar

100ml vegetable oil

50ml hazelnut oil

½ lemon, halved

The mayonnaise can be made 1–2 days in advance and stored in a covered container in the fridge until required. Put the egg yolk, mustard and vinegar in a non-reactive bowl and whisk to emulsify. Place the bowl on a kitchen cloth (to stop it from moving around) and slowly whisk in the vegetable and hazelnut oils. Season with a squeeze of lemon juice and salt to taste, then cover and chill.

Using a sharp knife remove all the sinew from the fillet, then cut the meat into fine dice. Place the meat in a bowl and place the bowl on top of a larger bowl or tray of ice. Season the meat well with salt and pepper before adding the apple, carrot, celeriac, chives, hazelnuts and shallots, and mix together. Add 1 tablespoon of the hazelnut mayonnaise and the vinegar and combine, adding more mayonnaise if needed.

I like to mould the tartare in a lightly greased metal ring for a stylish presentation, but it can also be simply spooned into the centre of a plate. Serve with a quail's egg yolk on top of each portion and a little extra cracked pepper.

Herb-crusted Venison Livers with Shallot Reduction on Toast

Liver and offal are what I call Marmite ingredients; you either love or hate them. But like with many things, I believe people don't like these because of bad childhood memories. I remember being served boiled liver at school and I didn't particularly like it. Venison liver and calves liver are both delicious but need to be cooked properly to enjoy. Getting your pan hot is really important here.

SERVES 4

---

4 venison livers, about 80g each, trimmed

olive oil

4 sourdough bread slices

4 teaspoons Dijon mustard

2 tablespoons chopped flat-leaf parsley and tarragon

sea salt and freshly cracked black pepper

For the shallot reduction

20g butter

olive oil

10 shallots, thinly sliced

1 garlic clove, finely chopped

1 teaspoon cracked black pepper

150ml dry white wine

100ml dry sherry

100ml Game Stock (page 279) or Beef Stock (page 278)

1 teaspoon wholegrain mustard – my favourite is Pommery

The shallot reduction can be made 2–3 days in advance and stored in a covered container in the fridge. Heat a well-seasoned sauté or frying pan over a medium-high heat, then melt the butter with a splash of the oil. When it is foaming, add the shallots and sauté for 2–3 minutes until softened. Add the garlic and pepper, and continue sautéing until they are tender.

Add half the wine and sherry, stirring to deglaze the pan, boil until they evaporate, then add the remaining wine and sherry and continue boiling until they reduce by half again. Now add the stock and leave the shallots to continue cooking for 10 minutes, or until most of the liquid has evaporated. Set aside and leave to cool completely, then cover and chill until required.

To cook the livers, pat them dry and season with salt and pepper. Heat a large well-seasoned sauté or frying pan over a medium-high heat, then add enough oil to cover the base of the pan. When it is hot, add the livers and fry for 1½ minutes on each side to colour. Remove them from the pan and set aside.

Meanwhile, toast the bread on both sides.

Add the shallot reduction to the pan you just cooked the livers in, stirring to deglaze the pan. Stir in the wholegrain mustard and adjust the seasoning with salt and pepper. Spread the shallot reduction on the hot toast. Brush the livers with Dijon mustard and sprinkle the herbs on top of each. Place the livers on the pieces of toast and serve.

Venison Escalopes with Parma Ham, Parsley and Shallot Butter

Making venison escalopes is a quick-and-easy way of showing the versatility of venison. You know the meat is going to be tender, but by battering and breading the fillet before pan-frying it crisp and golden, you get the lovely gamy meat with the crunch of the breadcrumbs. The Parma ham, parsley and shallot butter can be made in advance and chilled or frozen, ready for you to cut off slices when you need it – it's also good served on sizzling steaks.

This is great served with a parsley and shallot salad too.

— SERVES 4 —

60g plain flour

2 free-range eggs

1 tablespoon milk

100g panko or fine dried breadcrumbs

4 venison fillets, about 130g each

vegetable oil

4 lemon slices, to garnish

sea salt and freshly cracked black pepper

For the Parma ham, parsley and shallot butter

olive oil

25g Parma ham, finely chopped

2 shallots, finely chopped

½ garlic clove, finely chopped

4 tablespoons finely chopped flat-leaf parsley leaves

250g butter, softened

1 tablespoon ground almonds

1 teaspoon wholegrain mustard – I like to use Pommery

First make the Parma ham, parsley and shallot butter, which will keep in the fridge for up to 3 days, or can be frozen for up to a month. Heat a small well-seasoned sauté or frying pan over a medium-high heat, then add a splash of oil. When it is hot, add the Parma ham and sauté for 1–2 minutes. Add the shallots and garlic, season with salt and pepper and continue sautéing until the shallots are softened, but not coloured. Stir in the parsley. Pour into a shallow tray and set aside to cool completely.

Beat the butter in a bowl, then add the cooled shallot and parsley mixture, with the ground almonds and mustard, and beat together. Place the butter in the middle of a piece of clingfilm and shape into a cylinder, about 4cm thick. Chill or freeze until required.

Just before you're ready to cook, place the flour in a shallow bowl and season with salt and pepper. Beat the eggs with the milk in another shallow bowl, and place the panko in a third shallow bowl. Remove the flavoured butter from the freezer if it's frozen.

Butterfly each of the venison fillets by slicing in half horizontally, but not all the way through, so the halves stay connected. It should be like opening a book. Place an opened-out fillet between 2 sheets of clingfilm and use a meat mallet or rolling pin to lightly bash until flattened. Repeat with the remaining fillets.

One by one, dip the fillets in the flour to cover completely, shaking off the excess, then dip them in the egg mix and finally in the panko, patting the crumbs on well.

Heat a large well-seasoned sauté or frying pan over a high heat, then add about 5mm of vegetable oil. Make sure you get the pan really hot, because the escalopes need to cook quickly. When the pan and oil are hot, add the escalopes and fry for 2–3 minutes on each side until golden brown and crispy. Cook them in batches, if necessary. As each fillet is cooked, transfer it to kitchen paper to drain well and keep hot.

Wipe out the pan, then very quickly return it to the heat with add a little more oil. Add the lemon slices and leave for 1 minute on each side until they are caramelised.

Season the fillets with salt and top with a couple slices of the flavoured butter and a caramelised lemon slice before serving.

Smoked Venison Loin Rolls with Celeriac and Carrot Rémoulade

I often do this dish at home as a starter or even as a little canapé. All around the UK now we have some excellent farmers' markets and you should be able to pick up great smoked venison at one. Look online or in large off-licences for bottles of sugar syrup, which is often used in cocktails. Or you can dissolve caster sugar in an equal quantity of water over a medium heat, then leave it to bubble until it thickens to the consistency where it drips of a spoon. Just be sure not to stir once it starts bubbling or sugar crystals will form.

--- SERVES 4 ---

200g smoked venison loin in one piece
watercress sprigs, to garnish
olive oil for drizzling
sea salt and freshly cracked black pepper

For the carrot and celeriac rémoulade
100g celeriac
100g carrot
4 tablespoons Mayonnaise (page 276)
freshly squeezed juice of ½ lemon, or to
    taste
4 teaspoons very finely chopped flat-leaf
    parsley

For the blackberry compôte
300g blackberries, rinsed
100g sugar syrup
2 tablespoons freshly squeezed lemon
    juice
2 tablespoons full-bodied red wine

The rolls can be assembled and chilled for up to 4 hours before serving.

To make the rémoulade, peel the celeriac and carrots and use a mandolin or sharp knife to cut them into very fine matchstick strips, 6–7cm long and 3mm thick. Place them in a bowl, season with salt and pepper and mix with the mayonnaise, lemon juice and parsley. Set aside.

To make the blackberry compôte, put the blackberries in a heatproof bowl and set aside. Heat the sugar syrup, lemon juice and red wine together in a small heavy-based saucepan until just boiling, then pour over the blackberries and leave to cool completely. Transfer them to air-tight jars and refrigerate until required.

When you're ready to assemble the rolls, use a very sharp, thin knife to cut the smoked venison loin into 4 pieces horizontally, then cut each piece into 3 long strips.

Lay the venison strips on a chopping board and place a good spoonful of celeriac and carrot rémoulade at the end of each strip, then gently roll up to make bite-sized bundles. Cover with clingfilm and chill until you're ready to serve.

Serve the venison rolls with the blackberries and garnish with watercress leaves tossed with a drizzle of olive oil and seasoned with salt and pepper.

Venison Ragoût Lasagne

One of my wife Michaela's signature dishes is a smoked salmon lasagne and people often tell me how much they enjoy that dish. It got me thinking and I came up with this even better version of lasagne. The venison mince is very lean but the pancetta helps it stay moist, and the addition of pumpkin and chestnuts works really well. I think you'll find this is easy to make and very tasty on a cold evening.

SERVES 6

800g boneless venison haunch, chopped

200g pancetta, chopped

olive oil

2 carrots, peeled and chopped

1 onion, finely chopped

3 garlic cloves, finely chopped

2 celery sticks, finely chopped

2 juniper berries

1 bouquet garni

1 tablespoon tomato purée

250ml full-bodied red wine

600ml Game Stock (page 279) or Beef Stock (page 278)

300g pumpkin, peeled, deseeded and chopped

30g cooked chestnuts, chopped

200g spinach leaves, rinsed with any thick stalks removed

150g dry lasagne sheets

20g Parmesan cheese

sea salt and freshly cracked black pepper

For the béchamel sauce

60g unsalted butter

60g plain flour or chestnut flour

1 teaspoon Dijon mustard

800ml milk

1 bay leaf

2 teaspoons thyme leaves

The béchamel sauce can be made up to a day in advance and chilled until required. Melt the butter in a heavy-based saucepan, then add the flour and mustard and whisk for 2–3 minutes until a roux forms. Bring the milk, bay leaf and thyme to the simmering point in a separate pan, then gradually whisk the liquid into the roux and continue whisking over a gentle heat until the sauce thickens. Season with salt and pepper, then set aside. If not using immediately, press a piece of clingfilm on the surface to prevent a skin forming.

Use a mincer or a food processor fitted with a mincing blade and mince the venison and pancetta together. Heat a large well-seasoned saucepan over a high heat, then add a splash of oil. When it is hot, add the minced meats and stir until the mixture is nicely browned all over. Transfer the mince to a colander in the sink and leave to drain. You might need to cook the mince in several batches.

Wipe out the pan, then add a little more oil and heat over a high heat. Add the carrots with a pinch of salt and sauté until they are lightly caramelised. Turn the heat down and add the onion, garlic, celery, juniper berries and bouquet garni, and sauté for 3–4 minutes until the vegetables are softened. Return the venison mince to the pan, add the tomato purée and stir for 1–2 minutes to cook out the raw flavour.

Add the red wine, stirring to deglaze the pan, and boil until it reduces by half. Stir in the stock, cover the pan and leave the mixture to simmer gently for 20 minutes. Uncover and continue simmering for 40 minutes, or until the meat is tender and the sauce is nice and thick. Check occasionally and add a little water if it's too dry.

Meanwhile, heat a well-seasoned sauté or frying pan over a medium heat, then add a splash of oil. When it is hot, add the pumpkin with a pinch of salt and sauté just until it is tender. Remove it from the pan and leave to cool. Add the chestnuts to the pumpkin.

Wipe out the pan, then reheat it with just a small amount of oil. Add the spinach with just the water clinging to the leaves, season with salt and pepper and stir just until it wilts and is tender. Drain well, pressing out any excess liquid, then add to the pumpkin and chestnuts.

When you're ready to assemble and bake the lasagne, preheat the oven to 180°C Fan/200°C/Gas Mark 6 and grease a 2-litre ovenproof serving dish.

Spread a thin layer of the venison ragoût on the bottom of the dish. Add a layer of the lasagne sheets, then a layer of béchamel sauce followed by a layer of the pumpkin, chestnuts and spinach. Continue layering until all the ingredients are used and the dish is full, finishing with a layer of béchamel sauce and the freshly grated Parmesan.

Place the dish on a baking sheet and bake for 25 minutes, or until the top is golden brown and the filling is piping hot. Rest for 5 minutes before serving.

Venison Sausage Stew

This recipe is a bit of a family favourite. To my mind, it is a perfect mid-week supper, so when you have a bit of spare time make and freeze a batch, ready for a rainy day. I always enjoy cooking this dish with lovely root vegetables and apple, as the combination is unbeatable with the venison sausages. I also often serve this with a bowl of tagliatelle.

SERVES 4

olive oil
8 venison sausages
50g smoked lardons
200g celeriac, peeled and chopped
100g leeks, trimmed, chopped and rinsed
2 carrots, peeled and chopped
2 celery sticks, chopped
1 onion, chopped
1 tablespoon tomato purée
30g plain flour
250ml full-bodied red wine
5 juniper berries, crushed
250ml Game Stock (page 279) or Beef
    Stock (page 278)
1 bouquet garni
2 green apples
200g cooked chestnuts, halved
hot tagliatelle to serve (optional)
sea salt and freshly cracked black pepper

Heat a flameproof casserole over a medium-high heat, then add a good splash of oil. When it is hot, add the sausages and stir for 3 minutes, or until they are well coloured all over, then remove from the casserole and set aside.

Add a splash more oil to the casserole, if necessary, then add the lardons and sauté until they have rendered their fat and are well coloured. Add the celeriac, leeks, carrots, celery, onion and tomato purée, and continue sautéing for a further 1–2 minutes. Sprinkle in the flour and stir for 1 minute to cook out the raw flavour.

Add the wine and juniper berries, stirring to deglaze the pan, and boil until the wine reduces by half. Add the stock and bouquet garni, then return the sausages and any accumulated cooking juices to the casserole. Cover the casserole and leave to simmer over a medium heat for 20 minutes, or until all the vegetables are tender and the flavours blended.

Meanwhile, halve, core and chop the green apples.

Adjust the seasoning with salt and pepper, if necessary, then stir in the chestnuts and apples and warm through. Serve with fresh tagliatelle flavoured with freshly cracked black pepper.

Venison Stalker Pie

Venison stalker pie might be less well known than a classic shepherds' pie or cottage pie, but it's an ideal alternative for the winter months. I usually include celeriac and mushrooms to complement the meat, but the real secret ingredient is the Worcestershire sauce. Always use a floury potato for the mash topping to achieve a crispy finish.

— SERVES 4–6 —

vegetable oil

800g venison mince

80g smoked lardons

200g carrots, peeled and finely chopped

200g celeriac, peeled and finely chopped

200g button or wild mushrooms,
   trimmed, wiped and chopped

2 garlic cloves, chopped

1 onion, thinly sliced

1 teaspoon ground juniper

1 tablespoon plain flour

100ml port

100ml full-bodied red wine

300ml Game Stock (page 279) or Beef
   Stock (page 278), plus extra if needed

1 bouquet garni

1 tablespoon Worcestershire sauce, or
   to taste

sea salt and freshly cracked black pepper

For the mash

1kg floury potatoes, such as Maris Piper,
   peeled and chopped

150ml milk

30g butter, plus about an extra 15g
   melted butter for brushing

freshly grated nutmeg, to taste

Heat a large well-seasoned sauté or frying pan with a lid over a high heat, then add a splash of oil. When it is hot, add the venison mince and stir until it is well coloured and to remove any lumps. Transfer it to a colander in the sink and leave to drain.

Wipe out the pan, then return it to the heat with a splash more oil. Add the lardons and sauté until they have rendered their fat and are caramelised. Add the carrots, celeriac, mushrooms, garlic and onion with a pinch of salt, and continue sautéing for 2–3 minutes until the vegetables are beginning to colour and soften.

Add the ground juniper, sprinkle over the flour and mix well, stirring for 1 minute to cook out the flour. Add the port and wine, stirring to deglaze the pan and boil until they evaporate. Return the mince to the pan, then add the stock, bouquet garni, Worcestershire sauce to taste and salt and pepper.

Bring to the boil, then reduce the heat to low, cover and leave to simmer for 40–50 minutes, adding extra stock if necessary, until the mince is very tender.

Meanwhile, make the mash. Place the potatoes in a large heavy-based saucepan with cold water to cover. Season with salt and bring to the boil, then reduce the heat and leave to simmer until the potatoes are tender.

Drain the potatoes well, then return them to the pan. Add the milk, butter, nutmeg and salt and pepper, then mash and set aside.

When you're ready to assemble and cook the pie, preheat the oven to 180°C Fan/200°C/Gas Mark 6.

Place the mince mixture in an ovenproof serving dish and place on a baking sheet. Pipe or spread the mash over the top and brush with melted butter. Bake for 30 minutes, or until the mash is golden brown and the filling is piping hot.

Roasted Rabbit and Ceps

Ask any chef who worked at La Tante Claire, in London, for chef Pierre Koffmann about the staff food and I'm sure their faces will light up and a story will emerge … it was legendary! One of my greatest memories was the garlic-and-parsley-roasted rabbit legs and heads, which were absolutely sensational. For this recipe I've used the whole rabbit, minus the head, and I've added ceps. The spirit of the recipe is the same.

SERVES 4

---

2 rabbits, about 1.3kg, skinned, cleaned and jointed

vegetable or olive oil

100g ceps, trimmed and wiped

1 tablespoon finely chopped shallot

1½ teaspoons finely chopped garlic

1 tablespoon chopped marjoram

1½ teaspoons chopped flat-leaf parsley leaves

Dijon mustard, to serve

sea salt and freshly cracked black pepper

Preheat the oven to 180˚C Fan/200˚C/Gas Mark 6.

If you haven't bought the rabbit already jointed, use a sharp knife to remove the front and back legs and the head, and cut the saddle into 4 or 5 pieces, depending on size. Discard the head.

Pat the rabbit pieces dry and season them all over with salt and pepper. Heat a large well-seasoned sauté or frying pan over a medium-high heat, then add 2 tablespoons of oil. When it is hot, add the rabbit pieces and fry until they are well coloured all over. Add the ceps and stir for a further 1–2 minutes until they are well coloured.

Transfer the rabbit and ceps to a roasting tray and sprinkle with the shallot and garlic. Transfer to the tray to the oven and roast the rabbit pieces and ceps for 6 minutes, turning the pieces once after 3 minutes, or until the rabbit is cooked through and tender. Remove the rabbit and ceps from the pan and set aside to rest for 5 minutes covered with kitchen foil.

Just before serving, sprinkle the rabbit and ceps with the marjoram and parsley. Serve with Dijon mustard alongside.

Sautéed Rabbit Kidneys and Livers with Cavolo Nero

Italians and French absolutely love rabbit offal for its sweet taste. They love it so much you can buy the offal separately in the markets and supermarkets. Here, the sweetness of the offal works perfectly with shallots and pumpkin and the bitter cavolo nero leaves. This is a really different dish, but one of my favourites.

SERVES 2

300g mixed rabbit kidneys and livers

3 tablespoons olive oil

45g butter

250g pumpkin, peeled and diced

2 shallots, thinly sliced

4 teaspoons brandy

50ml whipping cream

1 tablespoon wholegrain mustard – I like to use Pommery

1 tablespoon chopped flat-leaf parsley leaves

1 tablespoon chopped sage

8 cavolo nero leaves, trimmed, blanched and kept hot, to serve

sea salt and freshly cracked black pepper

Prepare the kidneys and livers by removing any sinew and cutting the livers in half, then pat dry. Season with salt and pepper.

Heat a large well-seasoned sauté or frying pan over a medium heat, then add 2 tablespoons of olive oil. When it is hot, add the kidneys, livers and 30g of the butter. When the butter is foaming, spoon it over the kidneys and livers and fry them for 1–2 minutes until they are lightly coloured, but still pink inside. Remove them from the pan and keep hot.

Wipe out the pan. Return the pan to the heat and melt the remaining 15g of the butter with the remaining 1 tablespoon of oil. When it is hot, add the pumpkin and sauté for 4–5 minutes until it is beginning to soften. Add the shallots and continue sautéing until they are softened, but not coloured.

Add the brandy, stirring to deglaze the pan, and boil until it evaporates. Stir in the cream and continue boiling until it reduces and thickens. Stir in the mustard, then return the kidneys and livers to the pan. Adjust the seasoning with salt and pepper, then stir in the herbs. Serve with cavolo nero on the side.

Rabbit au Vin

Here I've basically swapped the traditional coq au vin for rabbit. I kind of imagined this recipe being cooked in a big cauldron pot on an open fire – but a large casserole works just fine at home. This is really good simple food at its best, and the root vegetable mash is a wonderful way of using up all the vegetables in the fridge.

When I get my hands on wild rabbit, this recipe is an extra-special treat. The cooking time is similar even though the wild animals are so much smaller.

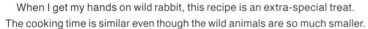

SERVES 4

2 oven-ready rabbits, about 1.3 kg, jointed
1 litre full-bodied red wine
6 garlic cloves, crushed
6 black peppercorns
4 carrots, peeled and diced
2 onions, chopped
2 bouquet garni
4 tablespoons plain flour
olive oil
200g smoked lardons
400ml Chicken Stock (page 279)
100g baby onions, peeled and halved
4 spring onions, trimmed
16 button mushrooms, trimmed and wiped
25g butter
sea salt and freshly cracked black pepper

For the mixed vegetable mash
160g carrot, peeled and diced
160g celeriac, peeled and diced
160g neep (swede), peeled and diced
160g parsnip, peeled and diced
25g butter
freshly grated nutmeg

Day 1
Place the rabbit pieces in a non-reactive container and pour over 500ml of the wine. Add 3 of the garlic cloves, 3 of the peppercorns, half the chopped carrots and onions and one bouquet garni, then cover the container with clingfilm and place in the fridge for 24 hours.

Day 2
Drain the rabbit through a colander and discard the flavouring ingredients and wine. Pat the rabbit pieces dry. Place the flour in a shallow tray and season with salt and pepper, then dust the rabbit pieces with the flour all over and shake off the excess.

Heat a large flameproof casserole over a medium-high heat, then add a good splash of oil. When it is hot, add the rabbit pieces and fry for 3–4 minutes until well coloured all over. Set them aside to drain on kitchen paper as they are coloured. Do this in batches, if necessary, so the temperature of the pan doesn't drop too much.

Add 150g of the lardons to the fat remaining in the pan and sauté until they render their fat and are coloured all over. Add the remaining garlic, peppercorns, carrots, onion and bouquet garni, and continue sautéing for 2–3 minutes until the vegetables are starting to colour and soften.

Return the rabbit pieces to the casserole. Pour over the remaining 500ml of wine and the chicken stock, season with salt and pepper and bring to the boil, skimming the surface as necessary. Lower the heat to medium and leave to simmer for 5–10 minutes, uncovered. Cover the casserole and leave the rabbit to continue simmering for a further 1½ hours, or until the meat is tender enough to flake from the bones. Check occasionally, because some pieces might cook quicker than others.

Continued on page 100

Meanwhile, make the root vegetable mash. Put the carrot, celeriac, neep and parsnip in a heavy-based saucepan, cover with cold water and season with salt. Bring to the boil, then lower the heat and simmer, partially covered, for 20–25 minutes until the vegetables are tender. Drain them well, then return them to the pan and use a potato masher to mash. Stir in the butter and nutmeg to taste, then season with salt and pepper. Set aside until required.

Just before the rabbit should finish cooking, heat a good splash of oil in a well-seasoned frying pan over a medium-high heat. When it is hot, add the remaining 50g of lardons and sauté until they render their fat and are coloured. Remove them from the pan and set aside to drain on a plate lined with kitchen paper. Add the baby onions and spring onions to the fat remaining in the pan and stir until they are coloured all over and tender, then set aside with the lardons. Add a little more oil, if necessary, then add the mushrooms with a pinch of salt and sauté until they are tender and have absorbed all the liquid they give off. Add to the lardons and onions and keep hot.

When the meat is tender, remove it from the pan and keep hot. Strain the cooking juices into a saucepan and boil until they are reduced by half. Stir in the butter, then adjust the seasoning with salt and pepper, if necessary. Discard the flavouring ingredients.

Meanwhile, reheat the mixed vegetable mash, if necessary. Serve the rabbit pieces, button mushrooms, baby onions and lardons with the reduced sauce spooned over, and the mixed vegetable mash alongside. Add a spring onion to each portion.

Fife Pie

According to legendary cookery writer Clarissa Dickson Wright's game cookbook, this is one of the earliest Scottish rabbit recipes. I've taken the traditional recipe from that book and modernised it a bit, but I've kept the great idea of making rabbit meatballs and putting them in a pie. It is really so important that old classic recipes continue to live on for the myth to continue! Well done, Clarissa.

— SERVES 4 —

vegetable oil
100g smoked lardons
2 carrots, peeled and chopped
1 celery stick, chopped
1 onion, chopped
50g button mushrooms, trimmed, wiped and chopped
6 thyme sprigs
1 canned anchovy fillet, chopped
freshly grated nutmeg
freshly squeezed juice of ½ lemon
320g puff pastry, thawed if frozen
plain flour for rolling out
1 egg yolk, beaten, to glaze
sea salt and freshly cracked black pepper

For the rabbit stock (makes about 900ml)
1 raw rabbit carcass
vegetable oil
10 tarragon sprigs
5 shallots, sliced
2 garlic cloves, crushed
100ml dry white wine

For the rabbit meatballs
15g butter
vegetable oil
2 garlic cloves, finely chopped
1 onion, finely chopped
50g button mushrooms, trimmed, wiped and finely chopped
1 teaspoon herbes de Provence
brandy
500g pork belly, skinned
400g boneless rabbit meat, diced
1 egg, beaten
2 tablespoons plain flour

First make the rabbit stock, which can be stored in a covered container in the fridge for up to 3 days, or frozen for up to 2 months. Chop the rabbit carcass into small pieces.

Heat a well-seasoned heavy-based saucepan or flameproof casserole over a high heat, then add a splash of oil. When it is hot, add the carcass pieces and stir until they are well coloured all over. Add the tarragon, shallots and garlic, and sauté for 1–2 minutes until the shallots are softened.

Add the white wine, stirring to deglaze the pan, and boil until it evaporates. Pour in enough water to cover the carcass and return to the boil. Reduce the heat, partially cover the pan and leave to simmer for 30–40 minutes, skimming the surface and topping up if necessary. Strain the stock, discard the bones and flavourings and set aside.

The rabbit meatballs can be made up to a day in advance and stored in a covered container until required. Heat a large well-seasoned sauté or frying pan over a medium-high heat, then melt the butter with a splash of oil. When the butter is foaming, add the garlic, onion and a pinch of salt, and sauté for 2–3 minutes until the onion is softened.

Add the mushrooms and dried herbs and continue sautéing until the mushrooms are tender and have absorbed the liquid they give off. Add a splash of brandy, stirring to deglaze the pan, and boil until it evaporates. Season with salt and pepper, then set aside and leave to cool completely.

Coarsely chop the pork belly. Place the rabbit meat, pork belly and mushroom mixture in a mincer or a food processor fitted with a medium mincing blade and mince into a bowl. Add the egg and season with salt and pepper. Fry a small amount in a well-seasoned pan to taste and adjust the seasoning, if necessary.

Lightly wet your hands, and roll the mixture into golf-ball-sized meatballs. You should get 16. Place the flour in a shallow roasting tray and season with salt and pepper. Add the meatballs and roll them around so they are well coated, then shake off any excess flour. Store in the fridge until required.

Continued on page 103

When you're ready to cook, preheat the oven to 200°C Fan/220°C/ Gas Mark 7.

Heat a well-seasoned sauté or frryin pan over a medium-high heat, then add a splash of oil. When it is hot, add the meatballs and gently stir them around until they are well coloured. Remove them from the pan as they are coloured and set aside. You might have to fry them in batches.

Wipe out the pan, then heat a splash of oil. Add the lardons and sauté until they have rendered their fat and are lightly coloured all over. Add the carrots, celery, onion, the remaining 50g of mushrooms and a pinch of salt, and sauté for 2–3 minutes until the vegetables are beginning to colour and soften. Add about 100ml of the rabbit stock, stirring to deglaze the pan. Add the thyme sprigs, then bring to the boil.

Place the meatballs in a 1.8-litre pie dish or a 25 x 17.5cm ovenproof serving dish. Add the vegetable mixture and 350ml of the remaining rabbit stock, or enough to cover all the ingredients. Add the anchovy, nutmeg and lemon juice to taste, and adjust the seasoning with salt and pepper. Place the dish on a baking sheet.

Roll out the pastry on a lightly floured work surface into a piece large enough to cover the top of the dish. Brush the rim of the dish with water, then press the pastry in position and crimp the edge. Trim any excess pastry and cut a small steam hole in the centre. Lightly glaze the surface with the beaten egg.

Place the baking sheet in the oven and bake for 30 minutes, or until the pastry is well risen and golden brown.

Remove from the oven and allow to stand for 5 minutes before serving.

Braised Rabbit Legs in Mustard Sauce with Tagliatelle

The key elements of this dish are the hind legs of the rabbit, as they braise so well and are full of flavour, a good-quality mustard (not the cheap stuff) and simmering the lovely rich, creamy rabbit sauce to the right consistency. Of course you can use chicken instead of rabbit and it will still be tasty, but it will not have that lovely mild, gamy flavour.

—— SERVES 4 ——

4 tablespoons plain flour

4 hind rabbit legs

2 tablespoons olive oil

2 carrots, peeled and chopped

1 onion, chopped

½ head of garlic

100ml dry white wine

500ml Chicken Stock (page 279)

1 bouquet garni

100ml double cream

1 tablespoon wholegrain mustard – I like to use Pommery

1 tablespoon chopped tarragon

hot cooked tagliatelle, to serve

salt and freshly cracked black pepper

Preheat the oven 140°C Fan/160°C/Gas Mark 3.

Put the flour in a shallow tray and season with salt and pepper. Pat the rabbit legs dry, then dust them with the flour and shake off the excess. Heat a flameproof casserole over a medium-high heat, then add the oil. When it is hot, add the rabbit legs and fry for 3–4 minutes until they are browned all over. Remove the rabbit from the casserole and set aside.

Add the carrots, onion, and garlic to the oil remaining in the casserole with a pinch of salt, and sauté for 4–5 minutes until they are softened and coloured. Add the wine, stirring to deglaze the pan, and boil until it evaporates. Add the chicken stock and bouquet garni and return to the boil.

Return the rabbit legs to the casserole and season with salt and pepper, then cover the casserole and return to the boil. Place in the oven for 1½ hours, or until the meat is tender.

Remove the rabbit legs and bouquet garni from the stock and set them aside. Add the cream and mustard to the pan and bring to the boil and reduce until the sauce is a good consistency to coat the back of a spoon. Return the rabbit legs and bouquet garni to the casserole and sprinkle with tarragon.

Meanwhile, bring a large saucepan of salted water to the boil. Add the tagliatelle to the pan and boil for 10–12 minutes, or the time specified on the packet, until al dente. Drain well.

To serve, divide the pasta among 4 plates, then serve with the rabbit, carrots and the sauce spooned over.

Braised Rabbit Legs, Red Pepper and Haricot Beans

Make sure you allow enough time to soak the haricot beans at least overnight or up to twenty-four hours. This hearty dish is full of flavour and has a massive influence from the south-west of France with beautiful rabbit legs cooked with the sweet red peppers, garlic, herbs, tomato and haricot beans. I love to keep the legs whole and serve one leg per portion on the plate, with the meat so tender it easily flakes off the bone as you eat it.

SERVES 4
---

olive oil

2 red peppers

200g dried haricot beans, soaked
    overnight in cold water to cover

3 tablespoons plain flour

4 hind rabbit legs

200g smoked lardons

4 garlic cloves, crushed

1 onion, chopped

1 tablespoon tomato purée

300ml full-bodied red wine

200ml Chicken Stock (page 279)

1 bouquet garni

chopped parsley, to garnish

sea salt and freshly cracked black pepper

Preheat the oven to 160°C Fan/180°C/Gas Mark 4. Heat a large well-seasoned ovenproof sauté or frying pan over a high heat, then add a good splash of oil. When it is hot, add the peppers and roll them around for about 10 minutes until charred. Transfer the pan to the oven and roast the peppers for 6–8 minutes until they are softened.

Transfer the peppers to a bowl, cover with clingfilm and leave for 5–6 minutes. Do not turn off the oven, but lower the temperature to 140˚C Fan/160˚C/Gas Mark 3.

One at a time, peel the peppers, then remove the cores and seeds and cut the flesh into strips. Set aside.

Meanwhile, drain the haricot beans. Put them in a saucepan of cold water to generously cover and bring to the boil, then boil hard for 10 minutes. Drain and rinse well, then set aside.

Put the flour in a shallow tray and season with salt and pepper. Pat the rabbit legs dry, then dust them with the flour, shaking off the excess. Heat a flameproof casserole over a medium-high heat, then add 2 tablespoons of oil. When it is hot, add the rabbit pieces and fry for 3–4 minutes until they are browned all over. Remove the rabbit from the casserole and set aside.

Heat another splash of oil in the casserole. Add the lardons and sauté until they render their fat and are lightly coloured. Add the garlic and onion with a pinch of salt, and continue stirring for a further 2 minutes. Add the tomato purée and continue stirring for a further 1–2 minutes to cook out the raw flavour and until the onions are softened. Add the red wine, stirring to deglaze the pan, then boil until it reduces by half. Add the chicken stock, red pepper strips, haricot beans and the bouquet garni, then return the rabbit pieces to the casserole. Bring to the boil, then cover the casserole and place it in the oven for 2 hours, or until the haricot beans are tender and the rabbit meat flakes from the bones. Check halfway through to see if you need to add more stock.

Adjust the seasoning with salt and pepper, then sprinkle with chopped parsley.

Braised Stuffed Rabbit Legs and Artichoke and Chorizo Barigoule

I was lucky enough as a young chef to work in the South of France and on my days off I would often eat in the old town of Nice, where I would find really great cooking at a good price. One of the brilliant Provencal dishes I loved in those days was artichoke barigoule, which I now serve with stuffed rabbit legs in this recipe.

When my produce provider rings to say he has got his hands on baby artichokes, I say give them to me! They are perfect for this recipe (use 12 in total) with its sunny Mediterranean flavours, but the season is so fleeting. For the rest of the year, I recommend using the more readily available globe artichokes.

SERVES 4

4 hind rabbit legs

400g crépinette (pork caul fat), rinsed and cut into 4 equal pieces

1 lemon, halved

3 globe artichokes

olive oil

150g fresh chorizo sausages

4 shallots, sliced

2 carrots, peeled and sliced

1 bouquet garni

50ml dry white wine

300ml Chicken Stock (page 279), plus extra if needed

fresh baby basil leaves, to garnish

sea salt and freshly cracked black pepper

For the stuffing

olive oil

½ onion, finely chopped

100g button mushrooms, trimmed, wiped and finely diced

1 garlic clove, chopped

1 teaspoon finely chopped rosemary needles

50ml dry white wine

300g pork belly, skinned and chopped

3 rabbit livers, trimmed and chopped

30g dried breadcrumbs

1 egg, beaten

25g fresh basil leaves

a knob of butter

First bone out the rabbit legs for stuffing. Insert a boning knife into the wide end of a leg, and cut around the thigh bone, pushing and scraping as necessary, down to the joint with the leg bone. Cut off and remove the leg bone, leaving the 'hollow' thigh attached. Scrape any meat off the exposed part of the leg bone and set aside. Repeat with the remaining legs – or ask your butcher to do this for you.

The stuffing can be made in advance and kept in a covered container in the fridge for up to 2 days. Heat a well-seasoned sauté or frying pan over a medium-high, then add a good splash of oil. When it is hot, add the onion and sauté for 3–4 minutes until it is softened. Add the mushrooms, garlic and rosemary with a pinch of salt, and continue sautéing until the mushrooms are tender and have absorbed the liquid they give off.

Add the wine to pan, stirring to deglaze, and boil until it evaporates. Set aside and leave to cool completely.

When the mushroom mixture is cool, mix it together with the pork belly and rabbit livers. Use a mincer or food processor fitted with a mincing blade to finely mince the mixture together, then put in a bowl and mix with the breadcrumbs, egg and basil leaves, and season with salt and pepper. Fry a small amount in a well-seasoned pan to taste, and adjust the seasoning, if necessary.

Divide the stuffing equally among the rabbit legs, stuffing the boned-out cavity in each leg. Wrap each stuffed leg in crépinette and set aside until you are ready to cook them. If they are chilled remove them from the fridge 15 minutes before cooking.

Just before you are ready to cook, prepare the artichokes. Squeeze the juice from half the lemon into a large bowl of cold water and set aside. Use your fingers to remove the outside leaves from one of the artichokes, then cut around the firm

Continued on page 110

heart to remove any remaining leaves and their bases. Cut off most of the stalk and slice across the top to reveal the inedible, pale yellow 'hairy' choke in the centre, rubbing the cut surfaces as you work with the other half of the lemon to prevent the flesh turning brown. Use a small spoon to scoop out all the fibres and discard them. Cut each artichoke into quarters, then immediately drop the pieces into the bowl of lemon water. Repeat with the other artichokes.

Pat the stuffed rabbit legs dry and season them with salt and pepper. Heat a large flameproof casserole over a medium-high heat, then add a good splash of oil. When it is hot, add the rabbit legs and fry for 2–3 minutes until well coloured all over. Remove them from the pan and set aside. Do this in batches, if necessary.

Add the chorizo sausages to the pan and stir gently for 2–3 minutes to release the natural oils. Add the shallots, carrots and bouquet garni, season with salt and pepper and sauté for 1 minute. Add the wine, stirring to deglaze the pan, and boil until it evaporates.

Add the chicken stock and return the legs to the casserole with the drained artichoke pieces. Season with salt and pepper, then bring everything to the boil. Reduce the heat to low, cover the casserole and leave to simmer for 30–35 minutes until the stuffed rabbit legs and artichokes are tender. If you insert a metal skewer into one of the legs, it should be hot when you put it to your lip. Check occasionally and add extra stock if needed.

Once cooked, remove the bouquet garni and adjust the seasoning. Garnish with baby basil leaves and serve.

Confit Rabbit Legs and Squid with Garlic and Parsley Risotto

This is not a difficult recipe, but you will need to get organised before you start. First make your rabbit leg confit and then make your chlorophyll. If it's your first time, you'll really enjoy the process. When you have both the legs and chlorophyll ready, start to cook your risotto. When it is about three-quarters of the way through, you can sauté the rabbit and squid, then finish the risotto and bring everything together.

SERVES 4
---

2 hind rabbit legs

200g coarse sea salt

500g duck fat, plus extra if needed

100g flat-leaf parsley, plus an extra 1½ teaspoons finely chopped parsley

200g squid bodies, cleaned, rinsed and dried

olive oil

1½ teaspoons finely chopped garlic

sea salt and freshly cracked black pepper

For the garlic and parsley risotto

800ml Chicken Stock (page 279)

90g butter

olive oil

½ white onion, finely chopped

250g risotto rice

100ml dry white wine

50g Parmesan cheese, freshly grated

a splash of sherry vinegar

First make the rabbit confit, which can be kept in the fridge for up to 3 days. Place the rabbit legs in a non-reactive container large enough to hold them in a single layer, then cover them with the salt. Cover tightly with clingfilm and leave in the fridge for 4 hours.

Rinse all the salt off the rabbit legs, then pat them completely dry with a kitchen cloth.

Melt the duck fat in a flameproof casserole large enough to hold all 4 legs in a single layer, but only heat the fat to 68°C, a temperature you can dip your finger into. You want enough fat to completely cover the rabbit legs, so melt extra if necessary. Add the rabbit legs and simmer at this heat for 2–3 hours until the meat is tender enough to easily flake from the bones. Remove the legs from the fat and set aside.

When the legs are cool enough to handle, remove the meat and discard the bones. If not using immediately, cover and chill until required. Just remember to remove it from the fridge about 15 minutes before the final cooking.

Meanwhile, make the chlorophyll, which will flavour and colour the risotto. Place the 100g parsley in a blender three-quarters full of water. Hold the lid securely in place and blend for 2–3 minutes until finely mixed. Strain this mixture through a fine sieve into a saucepan.

Place the pan over a high heat and bring to the boil, then immediately turn down the heat. The chlorophyll will rise to form a crust, which you can skim off and leave to drain on a double thickness of kitchen paper on a plate.

Use a very sharp knife to finely score the squid bodies on the inside in a criss-cross pattern, then cut into bite-sized pieces. Pat the pieces dry and set aside.

Continued on page 113

To make the risotto, bring the chicken stock to a boil, then lower the heat and keep it at a steady simmer. Heat another heavy-based saucepan over a medium heat, then melt 80g of the butter with 1 tablespoon of oil. When the butter is foaming, add the onion and sauté for 3–4 minutes until it is softened. Add the rice and stir for 1 minute so it is well coated in the butter. Add the wine and leave it to bubble until it evaporates.

Ladle in enough chicken stock to cover the rice, then stir constantly over a medium heat until it is absorbed. Slowly add the remaining stock, ladleful by ladleful, and stirring frequently for a further 15–17 minutes until the rice is tender, but still with a slight bite, or al dente. Season with salt and pepper.

Meanwhile, heat a well-seasoned sauté or frying pan over a medium-high heat, then add a splash of oil. Season the squid with salt, then add it to the pan and sauté for 1–2 minutes until it turns opaque. Add the flaked rabbit confit and the garlic and the remaining ½ teaspoon of chopped parsley and continue sautéing until the meat is hot.

When the risotto is cooked, remove the pan from the heat and stir in the green chlorophyll, the remaining 10g of butter and the Parmesan cheese. Taste and add a little drop of sherry vinegar.

Serve the risotto topped with the rabbit and squid.

Hare

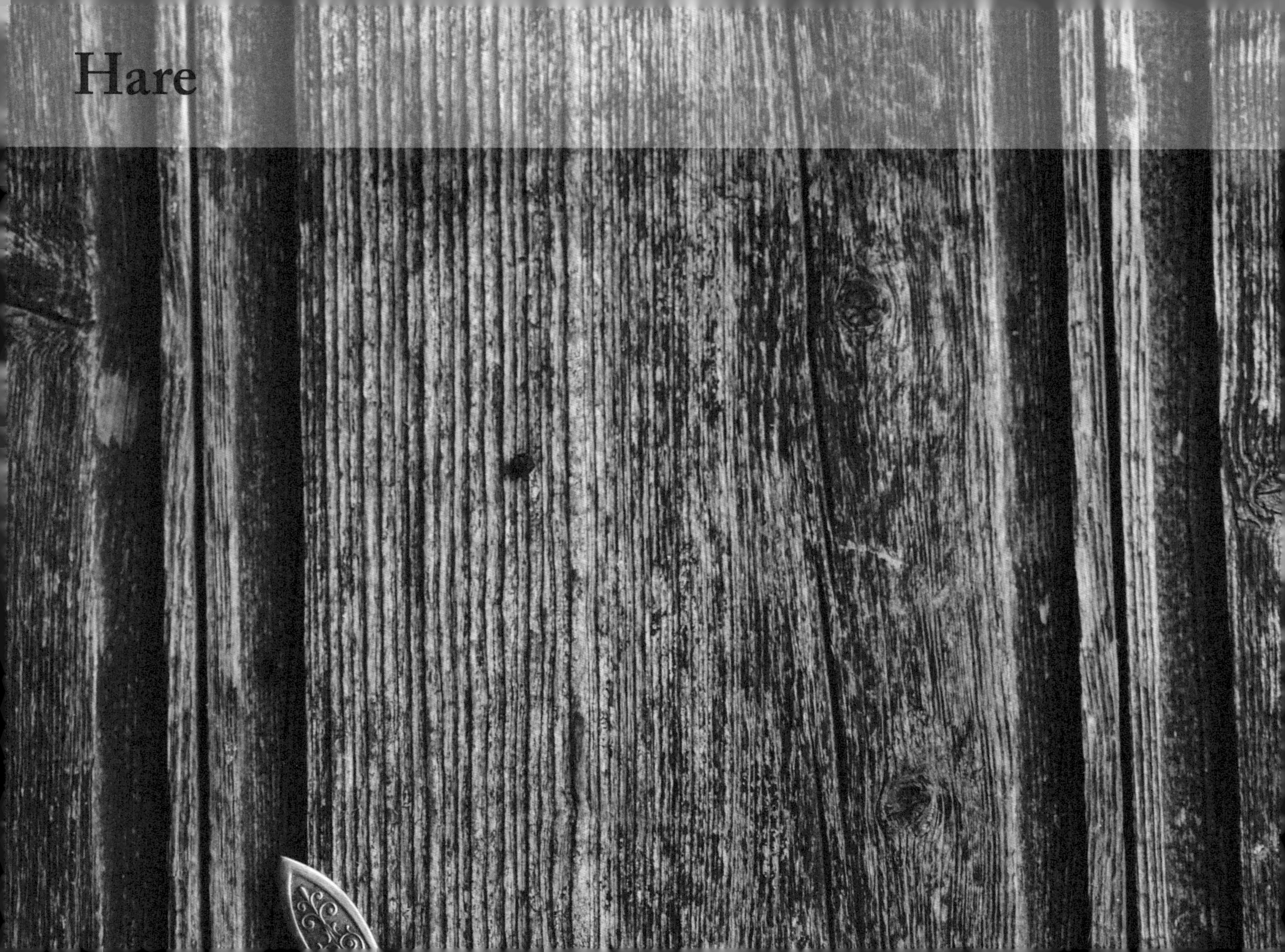

Roasted Loin of Hare with Beetroot, Celeriac and Turnip Gratin

Hare is usually associated with being very rich and often served braised or slow cooked. What many people may not realise is that the fillets are really easy to prepare and cook and not overly strong in flavour. It's great to cook them nice and pink like you would a piece of venison. I love to serve hare fillets with this root vegetable gratin, which is a brilliant twist on the traditional potato gratin but with the addition of beetroot for an amazing colour and flavour.

— SERVES 4 —

4 hare loin fillets, about 120g each
vegetable oil
a knob of butter
sea salt and freshly cracked black pepper

For the beetroot, celeriac and turnip gratin
½ garlic clove
20g unsalted butter, softened
400ml whipping cream
pinch of nutmeg
1 raw beetroot, peeled and very thinly sliced, ideally with a mandolin
½ celeriac head, peeled and very thinly sliced, ideally with a mandolin, and left in a bowl of cold water to prevent discoloration
½ turnip, peeled and very thinly sliced, ideally with a mandolin, and left in a bowl of cold water to prevent discoloration
2 thyme sprigs
1 bay leaf

To make the gratin, preheat the oven to 160°C Fan/180°C/Gas Mark 4. Rub the bottom of a gratin dish with the garlic clove, then generously butter all over the inside and set aside.

Put the cream in a small saucepan and bring to the boil. Season with nutmeg and salt and pepper, then remove from the heat and set aside. Drain the celeriac and turnip slices and pat them very dry with a kitchen cloth.

Place a layer of celeriac in the buttered dish, top with a layer of beetroot and then turnip. Repeat this layering, adding the thyme and bay leaf, until all the vegetables have been used, finishing with a layer of celeriac. Place the dish on a baking sheet, then slowly strain over the simmered cream so the vegetables are generously covered. Mop up any cream that spills on the baking sheet.

Place the baking sheet in the oven and bake the gratin for about 1½ hours, or until you can insert a knife without any resistance. If there is any resistance, put the dish back in the oven for 10 minutes. Leave to stand for 5 minutes before serving.

Just before the gratin is due to come out of the oven, season the hare fillets all over with salt and pepper.

Heat a well-seasoned sauté or frying pan large enough to hold the 4 fillets over a medium-high heat, then add a splash of oil. When it's hot add the fillets and colour on all sides. Add the butter to the pan, and when it foams baste the fillets.

Continue cooking the fillets over a medium-high heat for 3 minutes until they are well coloured. Set aside to rest for 3–4 minutes covered with kitchen foil.

Serve the fillets with the gratin and any juices that accumulated while they were resting spooned over.

Hare, Butter Bean and Chorizo Soup

This heart-warming soup has a real Spanish feel to it with the addition of butter beans and chunks of chorizo. Allow enough time to soak the butter beans for 24 hours before cooking, but if you want to cheat, tinned butter beans are not too bad as long as you rinse them thoroughly. I love to eat this with warm crunchy bread with a spreading of good-quality salted butter.

SERVES 4

300g dried butter beans, soaked
    overnight in cold water to cover
2 tablespoons vegetable oil
3 carrots, peeled and diced
1 onion, finely chopped
½ celeriac head, peeled and finely diced
½ leek, trimmed, thinly sliced and rinsed
1 teaspoon herbes de Provence
finely chopped parsley, to garnish
sea salt and freshly cracked black pepper

For the hare stock
2 tablespoons plain flour
1 oven-ready hare, cut into 4 pieces
vegetable oil
100g cooked chorizo, skinned and cubed
2 carrots, peeled and chopped
2 celery sticks
2 onions, halved
2 garlic cloves, chopped
150ml brandy
1.5 litres Chicken Stock (page 279)
1 bouquet garni

To make the stock, first put the flour in a shallow tray and season with salt and pepper. Pat the hare pieces dry, then dust with the seasoned four, shaking off the excess. Set aside.

Heat a large flameproof casserole over a medium heat, then add a splash of oil. When it is hot, add the chorizo and stir until it is coloured and has released its natural oil. Add the hare pieces to the pan and sear for 4–5 minutes until well coloured all over, then remove from the pan and set aside.

Add the carrots, celery, onions and garlic to the pan with a pinch of salt, and sauté for 2–3 minutes until they begin to colour and soften. Remove the chorizo pieces and set aside. Return the hare to the pan, then add the brandy, stirring to deglaze and pan, and boil until it evaporates.

Add the chicken stock and bring to the boil, skimming the surface as necessary. Add the bouquet garni and season with salt and pepper. Lower the heat, partially cover the pan and leave the stock to simmer for 2–2½ hours, skimming the surface as necessary, until the meat is tender enough to flake from the bones.

Meanwhile, drain and rinse the soaked butter beans. Transfer them to a saucepan with water to cover and bring to the boil, then boil for 45 minutes. Drain and rinse well and set aside until required.

Strain the stock through a fine sieve or chinois, then set aside the stock and hare meat and discard the flavouring vegetables.

To finish the soup, heat a large heavy-based saucepan over a medium heat, then add a good splash of vegetable oil. When it is hot, add the carrots, onion, drained celeriac, leek and the dried herbs with a pinch of salt, and sauté until the vegetables begin to soften.

Add the hare stock, butter beans and chorizo and season very lightly with pepper. Bring to the boil, then lower the heat and leave to simmer for 35 minutes, or until the beans are tender. Meanwhile, cut the hare meat into bite-sized pieces.

When the beans are tender, add the hare and heat through. Adjust the seasoning, if necessary, then stir in the chopped parsley to garnish.

Braised Hare Legs with Creamed Gnocchi

As with most game, the hare legs are very lean, so braising is one of the best methods of getting tenderness into them. The wonderful hare sauce that comes from cooking them with the red wine is rich and intense, which means the gnocchi works very well to soak up all the delicious sauce. Always roll the gnocchi when the mixture is still warm, as this will help to keep them light.

SERVES 4

50g plain flour
4 hind hare legs, skinned
olive oil
100g smoked lardons
4 garlic cloves, chopped
2 carrots, peeled and sliced
1 onion, chopped
½ celeriac, peeled and chopped
6 black peppercorns, lightly crushed
3 juniper berries, lightly crushed
1 bouquet garni
750ml full-bodied red wine
300ml Game Stock (page 279) or Beef
    Stock (page 278)
a knob of butter
 sea salt and freshly cracked black
    pepper

For the creamed gnocchi
300g rock salt
1kg floury potatoes, such as red rooster,
    well scrubbed with a nail brush and
    rubbed dry
1 large egg yolk, beaten
350g '00' flour, plus extra for rolling out
    the gnocchi
50ml Chicken Stock (page 279)
20g butter
3 sage leaves, thinly sliced
50g Parmesan cheese

First make the gnocchi, which can be made up to 3 hours in advance, ready for last-minute boiling. Preheat the oven to 200°C Fan/220°C/Gas Mark 7. Spread a thick layer of rock salt in a roasting tray large enough to hold the potatoes.

Prick the potatoes all over with the tip of a sharp knife, then rest them in the rock salt. Place the tray in the oven and bake the potatoes for 1½–2 hours, depending on their size, until they are very tender and a knife slides in without any resistance. Remove them from the tray and set aside.

When the potatoes are cool enough to handle, cut them in half and scoop out the flesh, then press it through a potato ricer or work it through a fine sieve into a large bowl. Beat in the egg, then gradually add the flour, mixing until the mixture forms a soft dough. It should come together and roll easily, but if it doesn't add a little extra flour. Knead until smooth.

Turn the mixture out on to a lightly floured work surface and divide into 4 equal portions. With lightly floured hands, roll each portion into a long rope, about 2cm thick. Cut into 2cm pieces. Roll each piece into an egg shape, then use the tines of a fork to roll back and forth to make the characteristic ridges. Cover with a damp kitchen cloth and set aside until you want to boil them.

Meanwhile, to cook the hare legs, let the oven cool down to 170°C Fan/190°C/Gas Mark 5. Place the flour in a shallow tray and season the flour with salt and pepper. Pat the hare legs dry, then dust them with the flour, shaking off the excess.

Heat a large well-seasoned sauté or frying pan over a medium-high heat, then add a splash of oil. When it is hot, add the lardons and sauté until they render their fat and are coloured all over. Add as many hare legs as will fit without over-crowding the pan and sear until they are browned all over. Remove them from the pan and drain on kitchen paper. Continue until all the legs are coloured, adding extra oil to the pan, if necessary.

Continued on page 122

Add the garlic, carrot, onion and celeriac to the oil remaining in the pan with a pinch of salt, and sauté for a further 2–3 minutes until all the vegetables are beginning to colour and soften. Add the peppercorns, juniper berries and bouquet garni, then pour in the wine, stirring to deglaze the pan, and boil until it reduces by half. Add the game stock and continue boiling until the liquid reduces by half again.

Return the hare legs to the casserole and season with salt and pepper. Cover the casserole and return the liquid to the boil, then place the casserole in the oven for 2–2½ hours until the meat is so tender it flakes off the bones.

Remove the legs and carrot slices from the casserole and set aside. Pass the cooking liquid through a chinois or a fine sieve into a heavy-based saucepan. Discard the flavouring ingredients.

Bring the cooking liquid to the boil and continue boiling until it reduces by half. Whisk in the butter and adjust the seasoning with salt and pepper, if necessary, and set aside until required.

While the sauce is reducing, bring a large saucepan of salted water to the boil. Add the gnocchi in batches to avoid over-crowding the pan and leave them to boil until they float to the surface. Return the water to the boil between batches. As they are cooked, use a slotted spoon to transfer them to a tray.

For the gnocchi sauce, bring the chicken stock to a boil in a large sauté or frying pan over a high heat. Whisk in the butter so it emulsifies. Add the sage to flavour the sauce, then gently add the gnocchi to warm through, basting with the sauce. Grate over the cheese. Adjust the seasoning if necessary, but remember the cheese is salty.

Meanwhile, add the hare to the sauce and gently reheat if necessary.

Serve the braised legs with the gnocchi on the side.

Hare Terrine

Okay, I agree, making a hare terrine is a big job to take on, but if you're going to do it there are no shortcuts. Once you get the hang of it, making terrines almost becomes therapeutic. From the first initial stages of marinating the hare to the final moment of truth of when you cut into the baked and chilled terrine, you're on a journey. Good luck.

MAKES 10 SLICES

---

1 hare

200ml full-bodied red wine, plus extra
    if needed

100ml brandy

6 black peppercorns

3 garlic cloves, crushed

1 bay leaf

1 thyme sprig

20g butter

1 tablespoon vegetable oil

1 onion, finely chopped

100g button mushrooms, wiped, trimmed
    and finely chopped

250g pork belly, skinned and finely
    chopped

100g pork fat, finely chopped

2 eggs, beaten

100ml double cream

20g dried breadcrumbs

30 streaky bacon rashers

100g prunes, stoned

100g ready-to-eat dried apricots

50g shelled pistachios

sea salt and freshly crushed black
    pepper

Begin this at least 3 days before you plan to serve, and after baking and overnight chilling it will keep in the fridge for up to 5 days.

Day 1

Ask your butcher to skin the hare, removing the head, heart, liver, kidneys and stomach. It should weigh about 2.1kg after evisceration. Next, remove all the meat from the hare, keeping the 2 fillets whole. Dice the leg meat and place in a covered bowl in the fridge until required.

Place both fillets in a baking tray and pour over the wine and 50ml of the brandy – they should be submerged, so add a little extra wine if necessary. Add the peppercorns, 1½ garlic cloves, the bay leaf and the thyme. Cover and chill overnight.

Meanwhile, heat a well-seasoned sauté or frying pan with a lid over a medium heat, then melt the butter with the oil. When the butter is foaming, add the onion with a pinch of salt, turn the heat to low, cover the pan and leave the onion to sweat until it is softened, but not coloured. Add the mushrooms and the remaining 1½ garlic cloves, turn the heat to medium-high and sauté until the mushrooms are tender and have absorbed the liquid they give off.

Add the remaining 50ml of brandy, scraping the pan to deglaze, and boil until it evaporates. Set aside to cool completely, then cover and chill overnight.

Day 2

Remove the hare fillets from the marinade and set aside in a bowl. Discard the marinade.

Add the pork belly and fat and the onion mixture to the diced leg meat, and mix together. Mince the mixture in a mincer or a food processor fitted with a medium mincing blade.

Return the mixture to the bowl and stir in the eggs, cream and breadcrumbs. Fry a small portion of the mixture in a well-seasoned pan to taste and adjust the salt and pepper, if necessary.

Continued on page 125

Meanwhile, preheat the oven to 160°C Fan/180°C/Gas Mark 4. Lightly wet a 32cm terrine (32 x 10.75 x 7.5cm), then line with 3 layers of clingfilm large enough to generously hang over the edges. Wetting the terrine first helps the clingfilm stick in position. (If you don't have the size terrine I specify, use a large loaf tin with a 1.2-litre capacity, and cover the mixture with a double layer of kitchen foil while it cooks.) Line the terrine with the bacon rashers, side by side crossways across the bottom and up the sides, again making sure they overhang the edges.

Season the hare fillets with salt and pepper.

Spread one-quarter of the minced mixture over the bottom of the terrine and pat down. Arrange the prunes in a row the length of the terrine. Spread over another quarter of the minced mixture, then top with the fillets, end to end. Spread over half the remaining minced mixture and arrange the apricots along the length of the terrine and sprinkle with pistachios. Spread the remaining mixture over the top.

Fold the overhanging bacon over the top, then fold over the clingfilm. Pierce the terrine top all over with the tip of a sharp knife and cover the top with the lid.

Place the terrine in a roasting tray and pour in enough boiling water to come one-third of the way up the side of the terrine. Place in the oven and bake for 1½–2 hours. To check is the terrine is cooked through, insert a metal skewer into the centre, then bring it up to your lip – if it is hot, it is ready!

Leave the terrine to cool completely, then place weights on top – tins of tomatoes and pulses are good to use – and chill overnight.

Day 3
Remove the terrine from the fridge, and invert on to a chopping board. If not using immediately, wrap in fresh clingfilm and chill until required.

Hare Suet Pudding

Suet puddings have a long history in British cooking, be it beef, lamb or game. This dish is a simple recipe to bring together, but the real patience is needed in giving it time to cook. Like with so many great dishes you have to be patient. Let it cook until the moment of turning out the golden pudding and cutting it to reveal all its glory.

SERVES 4

25g butter, softened, plus extra for greasing the basin

50g plain flour

600g boneless hare leg meat, cut into bite-sized pieces

vegetable oil

50g smoked lardons

200g button mushrooms, wiped, trimmed and chopped if large

2 shallots, chopped

1 tablespoon mixed chopped garlic and parsley

1 tablespoon tomato purée

200ml brown ale

sea salt and freshly cracked black pepper

For the pastry

450g self-raising flour

½ teaspoon fine sea salt

225g grated beef suet

330ml water

plain flour for rolling out

Butter a 1-litre pudding basin and set aside. Place the plain flour in a shallow tray and season with salt and pepper. Pat the hare pieces dry, then dust them with the flour, shaking off the excess.

Heat a large well-seasoned sauté or frying pan over a medium heat, then add a splash of vegetable oil. When it is hot, add the hare and fry until browned all over. Remove the hare pieces from the pan and drain well on kitchen paper, then set aside. Fry in batches, if necessary, to avoid overcrowding the pan, adding a little extra oil to the pan between batches.

Melt the butter with a little more oil. Add the lardons and sauté until they render their fat and are coloured all over. Add the mushrooms with a pinch of salt and continue sautéing until they are tender and have absorbed the liquid they give off. Add the shallots, garlic, parsley and tomato purée, and continue sautéing for a further 1–2 minutes until the shallots are softened and you've cooked out the raw flavour of the tomato purée.

Return the hare to the pan. Add the ale, stirring to deglaze the pan, and bring to the boil. Season with 1 teaspoon of salt and pepper to taste, then set aside while you make the pastry.

Sift the flour and salt into a large bowl, then mix in the suet. Make a well in the centre, slowly add the water and use your hand to work everything together until a soft dough forms, then roll into a ball.

Roll out two-thirds of the pastry on a very lightly floured surface with a lightly floured rolling pin into a 30cm round, 1cm thick. Drape the pastry over the rolling pin, then place on top of the basin and gently ease it into the basin, leaving an overhang. Roll out the remaining pastry into a round slightly larger than the top of the basin.

Spoon the hare and mushroom mixture into the basin, adding all the juices. Brush the overhanging pastry with water, place the lid on top and pinch the sides together, then trim the excess pastry. Cover the basin with pleated greaseproof paper that has been buttered on one side and kitchen foil before tying with string around the rim of the basin so they are firmly held in position. Place the pudding in a steamer and steam for 4 hours, checking occasionally and topping up with water, if necessary. Once cooked, remove the basin from the steamer and unwrap. Leave the pie to rest for 5 minutes before carefully inverting on to a serving plate and lifting off the basin.

Braised Hare Pasta Sauce

When we did the photo shoot for this book, we shared the food with the staff afterwards and this dish was particularly popular. Cooking hare in the pressure cooker is a brilliant way to give it a really wonderful rich tomato-y sauce. When using dried mushrooms, as in this recipe, remember not to throw away the mushrooms stock, but add it to the dish for extra flavour.

Do note, not all pressure cookers can be used on the hob so do check the manufacturers instructions for yours. If it cannot be used on the hob, I suggest transferring the ingredients into a normal saucepan.

— SERVES 4 —

50g plain flour
4 hind hare legs, skinned
olive oil
2 celery sticks, coarsely chopped
1 carrot, peeled and coarsely chopped
1 onion, coarsely chopped
100g dried ceps or morels, soaked in warm water to cover for at least 20 minutes
400ml full-bodied red wine
400g tinned tomatoes
1 tablespoon tomato purée
4 black peppercorns, lightly cracked
3 juniper berries, lightly crushed
½ garlic head, separated into cloves and lightly crushed
1 bouquet garni
sea salt and freshly cracked black pepper

To serve
freshly cooked hot pasta of your choice
chopped parsley
torn basil leaves
Parmesan cheese

This sauce is ready to use immediately, or it can be left to cool completely and then covered and chilled for up to 3 days, or frozen for up to 3 months.

Place the flour in a shallow tray and season with salt and pepper. Pat the hare legs dry, then dust them with the flour, shaking off the excess.

Heat the pressure cooker on the hob, then add a splash of oil. When the oil is hot, add the legs and sear until browned on both sides. Brown them in batches, if necessary, and remove from the cooker as they colour.

Add the celery, carrot and onion with a pinch of salt to the cooker, and sauté for 2–3 minutes until beginning to colour and soften. Squeeze the excess water from the mushrooms, retaining the liquid, and add the mushrooms to the vegetables along with the red wine, tinned tomatoes and tomato purée, then stir for a further 1–2 minutes to cook out the tomato purée's raw flavour.

Strain the mushroom liquid through a muslin-lined sieve into the cooker. Add peppercorns, juniper berries, garlic and bouquet garni. Return the hare legs to the cooker and season with salt and pepper, then seal it and leave to cook at Mark 1 for 1 hour, or until the meat is so tender it flakes off the bones.

Unseal the cooker and remove the legs and vegetables. When the legs are cool enough to handle, remove the meat from the bones and set aside with the vegetables.

Pass the cooking liquid through a chinois or fine sieve into a heavy-based saucepan. Bring to the boil and continue boiling until it reduces by one-third. Return the hare meat and vegetables and adjust the seasoning with salt and pepper, if necessary.

To serve, reheat and serve with hot pasta. Sprinkle with parsley and basil leaves and freshly grated Parmesan cheese.

Jugged Hare

There was no way I could write a chapter of hare recipes and not include the great classic of jugged hare. Yes, it takes a bit of planning and is certainly not your average dish, but wow what a dish it is. Hopefully with this recipe I've simplified everything to make preparation and process manageable, but make sure you get help from your butcher if you need it.

―――――――――――――――――――― SERVES 4 ――――――――――――――――――――

1 oven-ready hare, cut into 4 pieces with the blood, livers and heart reserved

2 bottles (750ml each) full-bodied dry red wine

400ml brandy

4 carrots, peeled and finely chopped

2 onions, finely chopped

12 juniper berries, lightly crushed

12 black peppercorns, lightly crushed

8 garlic cloves, chopped

2 bouquet garni

400g celeriac

200ml double cream

1 teaspoon red wine vinegar

100g plain flour

3 tablespoons vegetable oil

100g smoked lardons

400ml Game Stock (page 279)

8 baby onions, peeled

2 tablespoons chopped parsley

1 quantity Soft Polenta (page 232), hot, to serve

sea salt and freshly ground black pepper

Day 1

Place the hare pieces in a large non-reactive bowl or other container with 1 bottle of the wine, 200ml of the brandy, 2 carrots, 1 onion, 6 juniper berries, 6 peppercorns, 4 garlic cloves and 1 bouquet garni. Peel and chop 200g of the celeriac and add to the bowl. Cover the bowl with clingfilm and chill overnight in the fridge.

Meanwhile, prepare the livers and heart by removing any sinew. Place them in a blender or food processor with the blood, 100ml of the cream and a splash of red wine vinegar, and blitz until well blended. Transfer to a bowl, cover and chill until required.

Day 2

When you're ready to cook, preheat the oven to 170°C Fan/190°C/Gas Mark 5. Peel and finely dice the remaining 200g celeriac and set aside.

Place the plain flour in a shallow tray and season with salt and pepper. Remove the hare from the marinade and pat dry with a kitchen towel, then dust with the flour, shaking off the excess. Discard the marinade.

Heat a flameproof casserole over a medium heat, then add a good splash of oil. When it is hot, add as many pieces of hare as will fit without over-crowding and sear until coloured all over. Remove from the casserole and drain on kitchen paper. Continue frying the hare until all the pieces are browned, adding extra oil to the pan, if necessary.

Add 50g of the lardons to the fat remaining in the casserole and sauté until they render their fat and are coloured all over. Add the remaining celeriac, carrots, onion, juniper berries, peppercorns and garlic cloves with a pinch of salt, and continue sautéing until the vegetables are coloured and softened.

Add the remaining 200ml brandy, stirring to deglaze the pan, and boil until it evaporates. Add the remaining bottle of wine and continue boiling until it reduces by half. Add the game stock and continue boiling until the liquid again reduces by half. Add the remaining bouquet garni and season with salt and pepper.

Continued on page 132

Continued on page 132

Cover the casserole and return the liquid to the boil, then place the casserole in the oven for 2½ hours, until the hare is tender enough to flake from the bones.

Remove the hare from the casserole and set aside, trying to keep the meat in large pieces. I like to pass the cooking liquid through a chinois or fine sieve to remove any little bones, pressing down gently on the ingredients in the sieve to maximise the flavour and to thicken the sauce slightly.

Return the hare pieces and stock to the washed casserole. At this point you can leave the hare and broth to cool completely, then cover and chill for up to 2 days.

Meanwhile, make the polenta, following the instructions on page 232.

When you are ready to serve, heat a well-seasoned sauté or frying pan over a medium-high heat, then add a splash of oil. When it is hot, add the remaining 50g lardons and sauté until they render their fat and are lightly coloured all over. Add the baby onions to the pan and continue sautéing until they are tender and coloured. Drain well on kitchen paper and keep hot.

Reheat the hare and broth very gently. When the broth is hot, turn off the heat and slowly stir in the blended heart and liver mix, which will thicken the stew. It's important to do this off the heat, because if the sauce boils after the heart and liver mixture has been added it will split.

Serve with the polenta and top with the smoked lardons, baby onions and parsley. Add cracked pepper just before serving.

Hare Cannelloni

The variety of great pasta products available these days in good delis is quite remarkable. Of course it's always great fun to make your own pasta, like we do at The Kitchin, but there is not always time at home, so here I've used dried cannelloni tubes. I think this dish is a great way to get the whole family to enjoy eating hare (especially children), as its naturally strong flavour is mellowed with the cheese sauce.

SERVES 4

400g boneless hare meat

olive oil

50g smoked lardons, diced

2 carrots, peeled and finely diced

1 garlic clove, finely chopped

1 onion, finely chopped

1 tablespoon tomato purée

200ml full-bodied red wine

400g tinned tomatoes

1 bouquet garni

75ml water

Wilted Spinach (see page 276)

12 dried cannelloni tubes

25g Parmesan cheese

sea salt and freshly cracked black pepper

For the cheese sauce

35g butter

35g plain flour

430ml warm milk, infused with a bay leaf

100g cheddar cheese, grated – I like to
    use cheese from Mull

¾ teaspoon English mustard

The hare sauce for the filling can be made in advance, then left to cool and chilled for up to 2 days, or frozen for up to 3 months. Ask your butcher to mince the hare meat for you, but if it is too small of a quantity for them to do, mince it in a mincer or food processor fitted with a medium blade.

Heat a flameproof casserole over a medium heat, then add a good splash of oil. When it is hot, add the lardons and sauté until they render their fat and are coloured all over. Add the minced hare meat and sauté for 3–4 minutes, mixing well, until it changes colour. Transfer the meat to a colander and leave until well drained.

Return the casserole to the heat and add a little more oil. Add the carrots, garlic and onion with a pinch of salt, and sauté for 4 minutes, or until they are coloured and softened. Return the hare to the casserole with the tomato purée and stir for 1–2 minutes to cook out the raw flavour.

Add the red wine, stirring to deglaze the casserole, and boil until it reduces by half. Add the tinned tomatoes and bouquet garni, then add the water to the tin, swirl it around and add the water to the casserole, stirring. Season with salt and pepper and bring to the boil. Reduce the heat to medium-low and leave to simmer for 40 minutes, partially covered and stirring occasionally, until the hare is tender and the mixture is rich, but not too dry.

Meanwhile, make the cheese sauce. Melt the butter in a heavy-based saucepan over a medium heat. Add the flour and stir for 1–2 minutes to cook out the raw flavour. Slowly add the milk, whisking constantly to avoid lumps from forming. Simmer for 2 minutes, stirring, until the sauce thickens enough to coat the back of the spoon.

Remove the pan from the heat and add the cheese and mustard, stirring until the cheese melts. Season with salt and pepper, then set aside. If not using immediately, leave the sauce to cool completely, then press a piece of greaseproof paper on the surface to prevent a skin forming.

Continued on page 135

When you're ready to assemble and cook the cannelloni, preheat the oven to 200°C Fan/220°C/Gas Mark 7. Spread out the wilted spinach on the bottom of a 25cm ovenproof serving dish, then spread a thin layer of the hare mixture on top and spoon over a little of the cheese sauce. If you don't have the exact size dish, use one that will hold the tubes in a single layer.

Carefully use a small spoon to stuff the cannelloni tubes with the hare mixture, then arrange in the dish. Add the remaining mixture on top and pour over the remaining cheese sauce. Grate Parmesan cheese over the top and sprinkle with cracked pepper.

Place the dish on a baking sheet and bake for 35 minutes, or until the pasta tubes are tender, the sauce is bubbling and the top is golden brown. Set aside to rest for 5 minutes before serving.

Pot-roasted Chicken

I mean, who doesn't like a roast chicken? 'Pot roasting' just means you cook everything together in one pot, which maximises all those lovely flavours. The secret is to keep a good eye on everything, and insert a small knife into the vegetables periodically to test when they are cooked through because they cook at different times. I love how the vegetables take on the lovely chicken and garlic flavours.

SERVES 3–4

1 free-range chicken, about 1.3kg

olive oil

80g pancetta in one piece

16–20 small new potatoes, scrubbed

6 small red onions or shallots, peeled, but kept whole with the root on

4 carrots, peeled

4 thyme sprigs

3 bay leaves

2 heads of garlic, peeled and cut in half

50ml brandy

50ml dry white vermouth

300ml Chicken Stock (page 279)

15g butter

sea salt and freshly cracked black pepper

Preheat the oven to 200°C Fan/220°C/Gas Mark 7.

Place the chicken on a chopping board and use a small sharp knife to remove the wishbone, then tie the legs together with kitchen string for even cooking. Smear the chicken all over with olive oil and season well with salt and pepper.

Heat a roasting tray over a medium-high heat, then add a splash of oil. When it is is hot, add the pancetta and colour on both sides – this gives extra flavour to the dish. Remove the pancetta and set aside.

Add the chicken to the roasting tray on one side and leave it to turn golden brown, then use a roasting fork to turn it over and colour the other side. When it is golden brown all over, remove it from the tray and set aside.

Turn the heat down to medium, add the new potatoes, red onions, carrots, thyme, bay leaves and garlic, return the pancetta and season well with salt and pepper, then stir everything together. Use a wooden spoon or spatula to push the vegetables to the side of the roasting tray, and return the chicken in the centre.

Cover the tray with kitchen foil and place it in the oven for 60 minutes until the chicken is cooked through and the juices run clear when you pierce a thigh. All the vegetables and garlic might be tender before the chicken is cooked, depending on their size. Shallots will probably cook first so keep a good eye on them, checking after 15 minutes. When the tip of a small knife slides in without any resistance, you know they are ready. This is also a good time to baste the chicken with all the lovely juices. Wrap the vegetables in foil and keep hot as they are cooked until you're ready to serve.

When the chicken is cooked through, remove it and any remaining vegetables from the tray and set aside to rest for 5 minutes covered with kitchen foil.

Tip any of the cooking juices back into the roasting tray with the brandy and vermouth, stirring to deglaze the tray, and boil until they reduce by half. Add the chicken stock and continue boiling until it reduces one-third. Whisk in the butter and adjust the seasoning with salt and pepper.

Serve with the chicken and vegetables straight from the casserole.

Chicken en Papillote

Many chefs nowadays use the sous vide method of cooking ingredients in a sealed parcel in a water bath to guarantee succulent, flavoursome results, but I also like the somewhat old-fashioned technique of cooking in a sealed foil pouch in the oven. I think you also get consistently excellent results, and by placing the chicken into the foil pouch with the other ingredients the flavours are really intensified. The big wow factor of this dish comes when you place the puffed-up papillote on the table and then cut it open in front of your guest to reveal the surprise. This is a bit adventurous for a home cook, but certainly achievable.

This method is also versatile in that you can simply scale up the ingredients to serve more people. And, if you haven't made the lemon confit, use lemon slices instead.

SERVES 2

250ml Chicken Stock (page 279)

10g fresh ginger, peeled and sliced

5 lemon thyme sprigs

1 lemongrass stalk, outer layer removed and the stalk bashed

olive oil

1 carrot, peeled and cut into thin strips

1 fennel bulb, trimmed and very thinly sliced

½ leek, white part only, very thinly sliced

2 free-range chicken breast fillets, 150g each, skinned

20g Lemon Confit (page 277)

2 spring onions, finely chopped

sea salt and freshly cracked black pepper

The stock can be infused several hours in advance and chilled until you're ready to assemble the foil parcels. Put the chicken stock, ginger, 3 of the lemon thyme sprigs and the lemongrass in a saucepan. Season with salt and bring to the boil. Remove the pan from the heat, cover and leave the stock to infuse as it cools. When it's cool, strain the stock and discard the flavourings, then add a splash of olive oil. The stock can be covered and chilled until required.

When you're ready to cook, preheat the oven to 200°C Fan/220°C/Gas Mark 7. Cut out two 25cm greaseproof paper circles and place each one on a 42 x 30cm sheet of kitchen foil, shiny sides up. You need to cut out 2 more pieces of foil to fit over the tops of the 'cups' (see below).

Heat a large well-seasoned sauté or frying pan over a medium-high heat, then add a splash of oil. When it is hot, add the carrot, fennel and leek, and season with salt. Turn the heat to low, cover the pan and leave the vegetables to sweat for 3–4 minutes, shaking the pan occasionally to prevent sticking, until they are tender, but not coloured. Set aside and leave to cool.

Divide the vegetables between the greaseproof circles. Season each chicken breast with salt and pepper and place on top of vegetables. Sprinkle over the lemon confit and spring onions and add a thyme sprig to each parcel. Use the kitchen foil to help you mould the paper around the breasts, then gently divide the chicken stock between the 2 'cups'. Place the remaining pieces of kitchen foil on top, shiny sides down, and seal the parcels well so no steam can escape during cooking.

Carefully transfer the foil parcels to a heavy-based roasting tray. Place the pan over a medium heat on the hob for 4–5 minutes until the parcels start to expand, then transfer the pan to the oven and roast the chicken parcels for 15 minutes.

Serve the sealed parcel straightaway and open at the table for the theatrical effect.

Crispy Chicken and Curried Spelt Salad with Raita

This is one of the staff mealtime classics at The Kitchin – it's perfect food for busy people who need good wholesome food to fuel their appetites. It's really important you get the chicken skin nice and crispy. If any spelt is left over, use it the next day in a salad or soup.

SERVES 4

2 free-range chicken breasts, about 180g each
4 free-range chicken drumsticks
vegetable oil
coriander sprigs, to garnish
salt and freshly cracked black pepper

For the curried spelt salad

300g spelt
2 carrots, peeled and diced
50g shelled broad beans
50g shelled peas
2 tablespoons olive oil
1 onion, finely chopped
1 teaspoon ground cumin
1 teaspoon curry powder, mild or hot to taste
1 litre Chicken Stock (page 279), simmering
100g sultanas
1 spring onion, thinly sliced
1 handful mint leaves, chopped
extra virgin olive oil for drizzling

For the raita

½ cucumber
150g natural yogurt
2 tablespoons chopped coriander leaves
2 tablespoons chopped mint leaves

The curried spelt salad is served at room temperature, so it can be made in advance, covered and chilled until 15 or 20 minutes before you plan to serve so it returns to room temperature. Put the spelt in a bowl of cold water to cover and leave to soak for 5–10 minutes.

Bring 2 saucepans of salted water to the boil and set a large bowl of cold water in the sink. Add the carrots to one pan, return the water to the boil and blanch for 2 minutes, or until they are slightly tender. Drain well, then place in the cold water to stop the cooking. Add the broad beans and peas to the other pan and blanch for 2–3 minutes until just tender, then drain well and transfer to the cold water to stop the cooking. Drain all three vegetables well and set aside.

Drain the spelt and shake dry. Heat a heavy-based saucepan over a medium-high heat, then add the olive oil. When it is hot, add the onion and sauté for 2 minutes. Add the cumin and curry powder and stir for 1–2 minutes to cook out the raw flavour and soften the onion. Add the spelt and continue stirring to warm through. Season with salt and pepper.

Stir in enough stock to cover the spelt by 2cm and bring to the boil. Reduce the heat to medium and leave to simmer, uncovered, for 35–40 minutes until the spelt is tender, topping up the stock as necessary. Drain well and set aside to cool.

Stir the blanched carrots, broad beans and peas, sultanas, spring onion and mint into the cooled spelt, drizzle with olive oil and toss together. Set aside or chill until required.

When you are ready to cook the chicken, preheat the oven to 200°C Fan/220°C/ Gas Mark 7. Pat the chicken breasts and drumsticks dry and season with salt and pepper.

Heat a large well-seasoned, ovenproof sauté or frying pan over a medium-high heat, then add a splash of vegetable oil. When it is hot, add the chicken pieces, skin side down first, and fry until golden brown all over. Do this in batches, if necessary, adding extra oil to the pan as needed.

Continued on page 144

Turn the chicken pieces, skin side up, transfer the pan to the oven and roast the chicken breasts for 8–10 minutes until they are tender and the juices run clear if you pierce them with a small knife. Transfer the chicken breasts to a plate with a rim and keep hot. Return the drumsticks to the oven for a further 10 minutes, or until they are cooked through and the juices run clear when you test them. Add them and the cooking juices to the plate and keep hot.

Meanwhile, to make the raita, cut the cucumber into 7.5cm pieces, then halve and use a teaspoon to scrape out the seeds. Use a vegetable peeler to cut the flesh into ribbons. Put the cucumber in a non-reactive bowl, sprinkle with salt and set aside for 5 minutes to draw out the moisture.

Squeeze the excess moisture from the cucumber, then transfer it to another bowl. Stir in the yogurt, coriander and mint, and season with salt and pepper to taste. Cover and chill until required.

Serve the chicken on the spelt with the raita alongside. Garnish with coriander sprigs.

Chicken Terrine with Pistachio Pesto

If you're new to making terrines this is a good one to start with and a little more straightforward than the hare terrine recipe on page 123. In this recipe, I've simply put a cut breast and some prunes running through the centre, but as you get more adventurous you can also experiment with including other garnishes. I particularly like the pistachio pesto served with this. I borrowed the recipe from Sicily, where we holidayed one summer, and the unique twist is that you make it with an ice cube that helps set the green colour. Pistachio and chicken is a great match.

If you don't have the size terrine I specify, use a large loaf tin with a 1.2-litre capacity, and cover the mixture with kitchen foil while it cooks.

────────────── MAKES 10 SLICES ──────────────

15g butter

2 tablespoons vegetable oil

1 onion, finely chopped

100g button mushrooms, wiped, trimmed and finely chopped

2 garlic cloves, finely chopped

1 teaspoon herbes de Provence

1 tablespoon finely chopped rosemary

100ml brandy

100ml dry white vermouth

5 free-range chicken breast fillets, about 180g each

4 boneless free-range chicken thighs, about 160g each

200g pork belly, skinned and chopped

100g pork fat, chopped

25g chicken livers, trimmed and chopped

2 free-range eggs, beaten

100ml double cream

30g dried breadcrumbs

30 pancetta slices

100g prunes, stoned

sea salt and freshly crushed black pepper

For the pistachio pesto

1 garlic clove, peeled

large bunch of basil leaves

50g shelled pistachios, plus extra to garnish

50g Parmesan cheese, grated

freshly squeezed juice of ½ lemon

1 ice cube

5 tablespoons extra virgin olive oil

Begin this at least the day before you plan to serve so the terrine can chill and set overnight, but it will keep in the fridge for up to 5 days. The pistachio pesto will keep for up to 2 days in a covered container in the fridge.

Heat a heavy-based sauté or frying pan over a medium-high heat, then melt the butter with the oil. When the butter is foaming, add the onion and a little salt, turn the heat to low, cover the pan and leave the onion to sweat, shaking the pan occasionally to prevent sticking, for 3–4 minutes until softened, but not coloured.

Add the mushrooms, garlic, dried herbs and rosemary, and sauté until the mushrooms are tender and have reabsorbed the liquid they give off. Add the brandy and vermouth, stirring to deglaze the pan, then boil until they evaporate. Transfer the mixture to a large bowl and set aside to cool.

Preheat the oven to 120°C Fan/140°C/Gas Mark 1.

Finely chop 4 of the chicken breasts and cut the remaining one in half lengthways. Add the chopped chicken breasts, the chicken thighs, pork belly, pork fat and chicken livers to the mushroom mixture, and mix together. Finely mince this mixture in a mincer or use a food processor fitted with a mincing blade.

Return the mixture to the bowl, stir in the eggs, cream and breadcrumbs, and season with salt and pepper. Fry a small portion of the mixture in a frying pan and taste to check the seasoning, then adjust with salt and pepper, if necessary.

Lightly wet a 32cm terrine (32 x 10.75 x 7.5cm) and line with a piece of clingfilm large enough to generously hang over the edges. Wetting the terrine first helps the clingfilm stick in position. Stretch the pancetta slices with the back of a knife and then line the terrine with the pancetta slices, side by side crossways across

Continued on page 147

the bottom and up the sides, again making sure they overhang the edges. If you don't have the size terrine I specify, use a large loaf tin with a 1.2-litre capacity and cover the mixture with a double layer of kitchen foil while it cooks.

Spread almost half the chicken mixture in the terrine and pat it down. Season the sliced chicken breast with salt and pepper, then place on top in the centre, end to end. Cover with a thin layer of the chicken mixture, then add the prunes in a row down the centre. Top with the remaining chicken mixture and pat down.

Fold the overhanging pancetta over the top, then fold over the clingfilm. Pierce the terrine top all over with the tip of a sharp knife and cover the top with the lid.

Place the terrine in a roasting tray and pour in enough boiling water to come one-third of the way up the side of the terrine. Place the tray in the oven and bake for 2–2½ hours. To check if the terrine is cooked through, insert a metal skewer into the centre, then bringing it to your lip – if it is hot, the terrine is ready!

Leave the terrine to cool completely, then place weights on top – tins of tomatoes and pulses are good to use – and chill overnight.

To make the pistachio pesto use a large pestle and mortar to crush the garlic with a pinch of salt. Add the basil and pistachios and continue bashing until the mixture is paste-like. Add the Parmesan, lemon juice and ice cube, and keep mixing until the ice cube melts.

Slowly beat in the oil, then season with salt and pepper to taste. Transfer to a bowl and cover the surface closely with clingfilm. Cover and chill until about 15 minutes before required so it returns to room temperature.

Serve slices of the terrine with the pistachio pesto. Sprinkle over a few shelled pistachios, if you like.

Chicken and Wild Mushrooms in a Cream Sauce

I appreciate this dish might look a little cheffy, but it's a cracking recipe and not very difficult to pull off. Wild mushrooms in a cream sauce with chicken breast is a perfect combination and surprisingly quick and easy. Asparagus wrapped in pancetta not only tastes great, but also looks fantastic. Make sure you add the raw asparagus slices with a touch of olive oil, salt and pepper on top.

SERVES 4

---

olive oil

4 free-range chicken breast fillets, 180g each

20 thin asparagus spears, trimmed, with 4 set aside for garnish

8 pancetta rashers

20g butter

300g mixed wild mushrooms, such as ceps, girolles and oysters, wiped and trimmed

1 tablespoon finely chopped garlic

1 tablespoon finely chopped shallots

200ml dry white wine

250ml double cream

1 tablespoon very finely chopped parsley

1 tablespoon very finely chopped tarragon

1 teaspoon wholegrain mustard – I like Pommery

freshly squeezed juice from ½ lemon

sea salt and freshly cracked black pepper

Preheat the oven to 200°C Fan/220°C/Gas Mark 7. Bring a large saucepan of salted water to the boil and place a bowl of iced water in the sink.

Heat a large well-seasoned, ovenproof sauté or frying pan over a medium-high heat, then add a splash of oil. When it is hot, add the chicken breasts and fry until they are sealed and browned all over. Transfer the pan to the oven and roast the chicken breasts for 8–10 minutes until cooked through and the juices run clear when you pierce them with the tip of a knife.

Meanwhile, add the 16 trimmed asparagus spears to the boiling water and blanch for 1–2 minutes until just tender, then immediately remove and transfer to the iced water to stop the cooking. Drain them and dry them well with kitchen paper.

Divide the blanched spears into 4 bundles and wrap each with pancetta, leaving the tips exposed, then set aside. Cut the raw asparagus into thin strips to use as the garnish and set aside.

Heat another sauté or frying pan over a medium-high heat. When it is hot, add the pancetta-wrapped asparagus and fry for about 4 minutes, turning regularly, or until the pancetta is cooked and cooked and crisped. Set aside and keep hot.

When the chicken breasts come out of the oven, transfer them and their cooking juices to a plate with a rim and keep hot.

Return the pan to the heat and melt the butter with the remaining fat. When it is foaming, add the wild mushrooms, season with salt and pepper and sauté until they are tender and have reabsorbed the liquid they give off. Add the garlic and shallots and continue sautéing until they are softened. Remove the excess fat from the pan.

Continued on page 150

Add the white wine, stirring to deglaze the pan, and boil until it evaporates. Stir in cream and bring to the boil. Turn the heat to low and leave the mixture to simmer until it thickens and coats the back of the spoon. Stir in the parsley, tarragon and mustard. Adjust the seasoning with salt and pepper, if necessary.

Return the chicken breasts and any accumulated juices to the pan and re-heat, if necessary. Add the lemon juice and adjust the seasoning with salt and pepper. It's important to taste first though, because the cooking juices will be salty.

Quickly toss the raw asparagus strips with a splash of olive oil and salt and pepper.

Serve the chicken with the mushroom sauce and the pancetta-wrapped asparagus, garnished with the raw asparagus strips.

Chicken Confit Lollipops and Garlic with Raw Vegetable Salad

I'm sure you're probably familiar with duck leg confit, but chicken leg confit is equally good. If you slowly cook the chicken pieces in the duck fat a few days in advance they will be well preserved in the duck fat. It's really important to get the chicken skins nice and crispy, which is then set off beautifully by the raw vegetable salad. In the summer when fresh young broad beans and peas are ultra-tender you can even skip blanching them, and that is exactly when I love to eat this. It is associated with many happy memories.

SERVES 4

150g rock salt

11 garlic cloves, 3 crushed and 8 left whole with skin on

8 black peppercorns, crushed

2 thyme sprigs

1 bay leaf

8 free-range chicken drumsticks

800g duck fat

olive oil

For the raw vegetable salad

50g shelled broad beans

50g shelled peas

12 radishes

1 chicory head, separated into leaves

1 fennel bulb, trimmed and thinly sliced

1 radicchio head, trimmed and separated into leaves

6 baby carrots, cut in half lengthways

freshly squeezed lemon juice

First confit the chicken, which will keep in a covered container in the fridge for up to 4 days. Mix the rock salt with the 3 crushed garlic cloves, peppercorns, thyme sprigs and bay leaf. Spread half of this mixture in a non-reactive tray large enough to hold the chicken pieces in a single layer, then add the chicken pieces and top with the remaining rock salt mixture. Cover with clingfilm and set aside in the fridge for at least 5 hours.

After the chicken pieces are salted, remove them from the fridge and rinse off the salt and seasonings under cold water. Pat dry with kitchen paper and set aside.

To shape the lollipops, work with one drumstick at a time. Using a cleaver or large, sharp knife chop through the narrow top end of the drumstick to cut off the knuckle. Lay the drumstick on its side on a chopping board and chop a thin slice off the other – thicker – end to take off the bone. Hold the drumstick upright and use your fingers to push the meat and skin down towards the bottom to form the lollipop shape. The leg bone will be exposed and sticking upright, and you'll see the leg tendons sticking out. Use a pair of tweezers to pull out the tendons, then set the lollipop aside and continue to shape the remaining drumsticks.

Meanwhile, preheat the oven to 100°C Fan/120°C/Gas Mark ½.

Melt the duck fat in a large flameproof casserole or large ovenproof sauté pan until it reaches 68°C, a temperature you can dip your finger into. Add the chicken lollipops and the 8 whole garlic cloves in a single layer and cover the casserole or pan, using kitchen foil if necessary. Transfer the casserole to the oven for 1¾–2 hours until the chicken is so tender it flakes from the bone. Leave the chicken to cool completely in the fat.

Continued on page 153

Depending on seasonality and the tenderness of your broad beans and peas, you might need to blanch them. Bring a large saucepan of lightly salted water to the boil and place a bowl of iced water in the sink. Add the broad beans and peas and blanch for 2 minutes, then immediately drain and transfer to the iced water to stop the cooking and set the colour. When they are cool, drain them again and pat dry.

Add the beans and peas to the other salad vegetables and wrap them in damp kitchen paper until you're ready to serve. Ideally you should only prepare them about 30 minutes in advance, but they will keep crisp and fresh for up to 2 hours in the fridge.

About 20 minutes before you plan to serve, preheat the oven to 180°C Fan/200°C/ Gas Mark 6. Remove the lollipops from the fat and scrape off all the fat.

Heat a large well-seasoned, ovenproof sauté or frying pan over a medium-high heat, then add a thin layer of oil. When it is hot, add the chicken lollipops, and fry for 4–5 minutes until they are coloured all over and the skins begin to crisp. Be very careful as you turn them around.

Tuck the whole garlic cloves between the chicken pieces, then place the pan in the oven for 6–8 minutes until the chicken lollipops are hot. There isn't any need to add salt and pepper, as they are already seasoned.

Just before the chicken lollipops come out of the oven, place all the raw vegetables in a bowl, drizzle with olive oil, squeeze in lemon juice to taste and season with salt and pepper, then toss together.

Divide the salad among 4 plates and add the chicken lollipops and the garlic cloves.

Chicken Pie

As a father of four young boys, and with my wife working in the business, we are no different to any other family struggling to juggle our work life and family meals. That's why I always have a chicken pie in the freezer to pull out when needed. Just take it out in the morning and it will be ready to bake in evening. Of course, it's always that little bit better when freshly made, but all the flavours are still there when you've made it in advance, and my family really enjoys it.

— SERVES 6–8 —

25g plain flour, plus extra for rolling out

4 skinless free-range chicken breast fillets, chopped

4 skinless free-range chicken thigh fillets, chopped

olive oil

50g smoked lardons

250g button mushrooms, trimmed, wiped and quartered

2 carrots, peeled and finely diced

2 garlic cloves, chopped

1 onion, finely chopped

½ leek, trimmed, finely sliced and rinsed

1 teaspoon thyme leaves

200ml dry white wine

500ml Chicken Stock (page 279)

150ml milk

150ml double cream

1 tablespoon chopped tarragon

375g puff pastry, thawed if frozen

1 free-range egg yolk, beaten

seasonal green vegetables, to serve

sea salt and freshly cracked black pepper

Put the flour in a shallow tray and season with salt and pepper. Dust the chicken pieces with flour, then shake off the excess and set aside.

Heat a large well-seasoned sauté or frying pan with a lid or flameproof casserole over a medium-high heat, then add a splash of oil. When it is hot, add as much chicken as will fit in a single layer without over-crowding the pan and fry them until they are golden brown all over, then set aside on a plate with a rim. Do this in batches, adding extra oil as necessary.

Add the lardons to the pan and sauté until they render their fat and are lightly coloured all over. Add the mushrooms, carrots, garlic, onion, leeks and thyme, and continue sautéing for 3–4 minutes until the vegetables soften.

Add the white wine, stirring to deglaze the pan, and boil until it evaporates. Add the chicken stock, milk and cream, and bring to a simmer, stirring. Reduce the heat to low, return the chicken pieces and any accumulated juices to the pan and season with salt and pepper to taste. Leave to simmer, covered, for 35–40 minutes until the chicken is tender and cooked through. Stir in the tarragon and season with salt and pepper. When the chicken is tender, transfer it and the cream sauce to a 2-litre ovenproof dish.

Roll out the pastry on a lightly floured surface with a lightly floured rolling pin until it is about 2cm thick. Cut a strip of pastry the same width as the rim of your pie dish. Lightly brush the edge of the dish with egg yolk and fix the strip around it. Brush the top of the pastry strip with egg yolk, then lay over the remaining pastry and press down lightly. Cut off the excess pastry to trim the edge, then crimp. Use a small knife to cut a steam hole in the centre and insert a foil funnel to let the steam escape during baking. Cut any pastry trimmings into leaves and secure them to the surface with egg yolk and glaze, if you like. Transfer the pie to the fridge to chill for 20 minutes.

Meanwhile, preheat the oven to 200°C Fan/220°C/Gas Mark 7.

Glaze the surface of the pie with the remaining beaten egg yolk. Place the pie on a baking sheet and bake for 30 minutes, or until the filling is bubbling and the pastry is golden brown. Once cooked, remove from the oven and leave to rest for 5 minutes before serving.

Blackened Chicken Tacos with Avocado and Pea Guacamole

This is a Kitchin family movie supper classic – something fun to eat while we all settle down in front of the screen. I was lucky enough to spend time in Barbados a few years ago and I fell in love with the chicken and blackened spice combo. The avocado with peas is something I picked up in a New York Mexican restaurant later, but it works incredibly well with the chicken, and that's how this recipe has evolved into a Kitchin family favourite.

MAKES 12

4 free-range chicken breast fillets, each
    cut into 5 strips
100g Cajun spice mix
olive oil
sea salt

For the avocado and pea guacamole
200g frozen peas
olive oil
finely grated zest and juice of 1 lime
3 ripe avocados
2 small green chillies, deseeded and very
    finely chopped
2 spring onions, finely chopped

For the tomato salsa
200g cherry tomatoes, chopped
½ green chilli, deseeded and chopped
1 tablespoon finely chopped shallot

To serve
1 Baby Gem lettuce, shredded
100g crème fraîche
12 small tacos shells
 sunflower seeds

Place the chicken strips in a non-reactive bowl and add a good sprinkling of spice mix and a splash of olive oil – the spicier you like your food, the more spice mix you should use. Season lightly with salt, then set aside for 30 minutes.

Meanwhile, make the guacamole. Bring a saucepan of lightly salted water to the boil and set a bowl of iced water in the sink. Add the frozen peas to the boiling water and blanch for 3–5 minutes until tender. Drain them well, then tip them into the iced water to stop the cooking and set the colour.

Drain the peas again and transfer to a blender or food processor with about 2 tablespoons of oil, the lime zest and juice and a splash of water. Season with salt and blend to make a chunky purée. Set aside.

Halve the avocados, remove the stones and peel them. Put the flesh in a non-reactive bowl and use a fork to coarsely mash. Add the pea purée, green chillies and spring onions, and season with salt. Cover the surface closely with clingfilm and chill for up to 2 hours until required.

To make the tomato salsa, put all the ingredients in a non-reactive bowl and season with salt and pepper. Set aside until required.

When you're ready to cook the chicken, heat a large well-seasoned sauté or frying pan over a medium-high heat, then brush the surface with oil. When it is hot, add as many chicken strips as will fit without over-crowding the pan and fry, turning once, for 4 minutes, until they are cooked through and tender. Cook in batches, adding a little extra oil, if necessary. Remove the chicken from the pan and keep hot.

To serve, divide the shredded lettuce among the taco shells. Top each with a couple of spoonfuls of guacamole, followed by chicken. Add the tomato salsa and a dollop of crème fraîche to each, then sprinkle with sunflower seeds and serve.

Roast Pheasant with a Cabbage and Apple Salad

Making the herb-flavoured butter is fun and easy, and you can make it in advance and freeze. Using flavoured butter is a great technique to get lots of flavour into many dishes. In this one, however, you have to be careful not to rip the pheasant's skin when you use your fingers to ease the butter over the breasts.

SERVES 2

1 oven-ready pheasant, about 600g

olive oil

sea salt and freshly cracked black pepper

For the herb butter

200g butter, diced

4 tablespoons flat-leaf parsley leaves

10 tarragon sprigs

10 chervil sprigs

10 rosemary sprigs

1 garlic clove, very finely chopped

finely grated zest of 1 lemon

2 teaspoons cracked black peppercorns

For the cabbage and apple salad

1 small savoy cabbage, or 1 large savoy
    cabbage heart

olive oil

50g smoked lardons

½ green apple

½ red apple

balsamic vinegar

flat-leaf parsley leaves, to garnish

First make the herb butter, which should be frozen for at least 2 hours, but will keep for up to 3 weeks in the freezer. Melt the butter in a small saucepan, then set aside and leave until cool and just starting to set. You don't want it to set firmly.

Line a shallow baking tray or freezerproof dish that will fit in your freezer with greaseproof paper. Pick all the herbs from the stalks and place in a blender. Whizz a few times to cut the herbs without overmixing, or they will get bashed. (Alternatively, just finely chop the herbs with a knife.) Add the herbs, garlic, lemon zest and peppercorns to the melted butter, and season with salt. Pour the mixture into the prepared tray and freeze for at least 2 hours, or until required.

When ready to cook, preheat the oven to 200°C Fan/220°C/Gas Mark 7.

Being careful to avoid ripping the skin, slide your fingers under the pheasant's skin, starting at the neck, to ease it away from the breasts and upper part of the legs. Remove the butter from the freezer and break off pieces, then slide them under the skin. Use the palm of your hand and your fingers on top of the skin to spread the butter all over the bird. Truss the bird with kitchen string. Season the bird all over with salt and pepper. (Wrap leftover butter in greaseproof paper and freeze – it's very good to add to pan-fried steaks, too.)

Heat a large well-seasoned, ovenproof sauté or frying pan over a high heat, then add a thin layer of oil. When it is hot, add the pheasant and brown all over. Transfer the pan to the oven and roast the pheasant, basting occasionally, for 25–30 minutes, depending on the size, until tender and the juices run clear when you pierce the thigh with a skewer. Set aside to rest for 5 minutes covered with kitchen foil.

Meanwhile, start the salad. Cut off the root end of the cabbage, then cut the cabbage in half and carefully cut out the thick veins that run through the leaves. Finely shred the leaves and set aside.

Heat a small well-seasoned sauté or frying pan over a medium heat, then add a splash of oil. When it is hot, add the lardons and sauté until they are crispy. Transfer them to kitchen paper and leave to cool.

While the pheasant is resting, halve, core and cut the apples into chunks at the last minute so they don't discolour. Combine the cabbage, apple chunks and lardons. Season with salt and pepper, then add olive oil and balsamic vinegar to taste and toss together.

Carve the pheasant and spoon over the accumulated juices, then serve with the cabbage and apple salad.

Potted Pheasant

I have often heard people mentioning they have been given a brace of pheasants as a gift, but the birds have ended up in the freezer, because they don't know what to do with them. If that's ever the case with you, this is a brilliant recipe to use them up, and it keeps really well in the fridge once in the jars. The pheasant is really delicious on toast with gherkins and maybe a sneaky glass of cider, which is often how our grandparents used to enjoy this dish.

SERVES 4

1 oven-ready pheasant, about 600g

75g rock salt

1kg duck fat

300g pork belly in 1 piece

4 juniper berries

3 garlic cloves, chopped

3 thyme sprigs

2 bay leaves

2 rosemary sprigs

50g gherkins, drained and finely chopped, plus extra to serve

1 tablespoon chopped flat-leaf parsley

1 teaspoon dried pink peppercorns, to garnish

French bread, to serve

sea salt and freshly cracked black pepper

Using a sharp knife, remove the legs, breast and skin from the pheasant, then separate the legs and thighs. Cut the breasts in to chunks. (Keep the carcass to make a stock. If you don't want to do that immediately, the bones can be frozen until you're in the mood or have time.)

Dust the pheasant pieces with the rock salt, then cover with clingfilm and place in the fridge for 1½–2 hours.

When ready to cook, preheat the oven to 120°C Fan/140°C/Gas Mark 1. Meanwhile, remove the pheasant from the fridge and rinse off the salt under cold running water and dry well with a kitchen cloth.

Heat a flameproof casserole over a medium heat, then add the duck fat. When it melts, add the pheasant pieces and pork belly and warm them gently. Stir in the juniper berries, garlic, thyme, bay leaves and rosemary sprigs. Cover the casserole and place in the oven for 2–2½ hours until the pheasant is tender enough to flake from the bones.

Remove the pheasant and pork from the casserole and set aside. When they are cool enough to handle, remove the pheasant skin and flake the meat off the bones into a bowl. Be extra careful not to include any of the small leg bones. Remove the skin from the pork belly and shred the meat into the bowl. Add 5 teaspoons of the duck fat, the gherkins and parsley, and mix well.

Season the pheasant mixture with salt and pepper. Transfer to Kilner or other preserving jars and pour over enough remaining fat to make an airtight seal. As the fat starts to set, sprinkle with pink peppercorns and cracked black pepper. Leave to cool completely, then close the jar and transfer to the fridge for up to 5 days.

Serve a jar of potted pheasant with bread and extra gherkins on the side, if you like.

Asian Poached Pheasant

This recipe brings together a traditionally British game bird with Far Eastern flavours, and it's an incredibly healthy meal as it's low in fat. Poaching the pheasant this way also keeps the meat lovely and moist. This is one of those dishes that leave you feeling revitalised, rather than too full.

SERVES 2

---

2 pheasant breasts, skinned, boned and all sinew removed

600ml Game Stock (page 279) or Chicken Stock (page 279)

1 fennel bulb, trimmed and sliced

1 lemongrass stalk, outer layer removed, stalk bashed and cut in half lengthways

2 teaspoons peeled and thinly sliced root ginger

1 teaspoon coriander seeds

1 teaspoon fennel seeds

½–1 fresh red chilli (depending on how spicy you like your food) sliced, to serve

chopped coriander sprigs, to serve

sea salt and freshly cracked black pepper

Season the pheasant breasts all over with salt and pepper, then set aside.

Heat a heavy-based saucepan over a high heat. Add the stock, fennel, lemongrass, ginger and coriander and fennel seeds. Season with salt and pepper and bring to the boil, then lower the heat. Add the pheasant breasts to the stock and poach for 8–12 minutes, depending on their size, until tender. Remove the breasts from the pan and cut each one into 4 pieces.

Add the chilli and chopped coriander to the broth and adjust the seasoning with salt and pepper, if necessary. Return the pheasant meat to pan and warm through, if necessary, then serve.

Pheasant Cock-a-Leekie

Cock-a-leekie is one of the classic dishes of Scottish cooking, but is traditionally made with chicken. Don't cut any corners by not putting prunes in, as they work fantastically well with the pheasant. This is a proper 'do-you-good soup' that will keep you going throughout the day.

— SERVES 4 —

1 oven-ready pheasant, about 600g, cut into pieces
olive oil
150g smoked lardons
2 celery sticks, chopped
2 leeks, trimmed, sliced and rinsed
2 onions, chopped
100ml dry white wine
1.5 litres water
1 bouquet garni
200g basmati rice
100g prunes, halved and stoned, to serve
chopped flat-leaf parsley, to garnish
salt and freshly cracked black pepper

Pat the pheasant pieces dry, then season them with salt and pepper. Heat a large heavy-based saucepan over a medium-high heat, then add a good splash of oil. When it is hot, add the pheasant pieces and sauté for 2–3 minutes until they are starting to colour. Remove them from the pan and set aside.

Reheat the pan with any remaining fat. Add the lardons and sauté until they render their fat and are coloured all over. Stir in half of the celery, leeks and onions, and continue sautéing for 2–3 minutes until they are beginning to colour and soften. Add the wine, stirring to deglaze the pan, and boil until it evaporates.

Return the pheasant pieces to the pan with the water and bouquet garni. Add extra water, if necessary, so all the ingredients are submerged. Slowly bring to the boil, skimming the surface. Reduce the heat to low, season with salt and pepper, partially cover and leave to simmer for 40–45 minutes until the pheasant breasts are tender and the broth is flavoursome.

Meanwhile, rinse the rice under cold running water until the water runs clear, then set aside.

Strain the broth through a chinois or fine sieve, then return it to the washed pan. Set the pheasant pieces aside, and discard the flavouring vegetables, lardons and bouquet garni.

Bring the broth to the boil, add the rice and remaining celery, leek and onion, and leave to lightly boil for 8–10 minutes until the rice and vegetables are tender, adding extra water if necessary.

When the pheasant pieces are cool enough to handle, remove the skin and pull the meat from the bones, tearing into bite-sized pieces. (Keep the carcasses to make a stock. If you don't want to do that immediately, the bones can be frozen until you're in the mood or have time.) Once the rice and vegetables are tender, return the pheasant meat to the broth to gently reheat. Adjust the seasoning with salt and pepper.

When ready to serve, stir in the prunes, heat through, then ladle into bowls and sprinkle with parsley.

Pheasant Breasts with Jerusalem Artichoke and Pearl Barley Risotto

This recipe is a perfect mid-week supper recipe, and pearl barley makes a great alternative to the traditional risotto rice. I love the texture it keeps when it's cooked. Here I've used Jerusalem artichokes, which gives such a lovely nutty flavour to the dish. The key is not to season the pheasant too much, as it's wrapped in pancetta, which is quite salty itself.

―――――――――――――――――― SERVES 2 ――――――――――――――――――

10 pancetta slices
2 pheasant breasts, skinned
olive oil
salt and freshly cracked black pepper

For the Jerusalem artichoke and pearl barley risotto
freshly squeezed juice of ½ lemon
250g Jerusalem artichokes
2 tablespoons olive oil
200g pearl barley, soaked in cold water to cover for 1 hour
25g butter
1 small white onion, finely chopped
50ml dry white wine
500ml Chicken Stock (page 279), simmering
50g Parmesan cheese, freshly grated
2 tablespoons whipping cream
1 tablespoon finely chopped flat-leaf parsley
splash of sherry vinegar

Up to 1 or 2 hours in advance, arrange 5 overlapping pancetta slices side by side on a sheet of clingfilm so they are the length of a pheasant breast. Lightly season a breast with salt and pepper, but remember the pancetta can be salty. Place the breast across the pancetta, then wrap the pancetta around the breast so it is completely enclosed. Wrap the clingfilm around the meat and tightly twist the ends to make a smooth, neat cylinder. Repeat with the remaining pancetta and breast. Place in the fridge for 1–2 hours until 15 minutes before you plan to cook so they return to room temperature.

To cook the Jerusalem artichokes, preheat the oven to 200°C Fan/220°C/Gas Mark 7 and add the lemon juice to a large bowl of water. Peel the Jerusalem artichokes, then cut each into 4 or 6 pieces, dropping the pieces into the lemon water to prevent discolouration. When all are prepared, drain them and pat dry.

Heat a large well-seasoned, ovenproof sauté or frying pan over a medium-high heat, then add 1 tablespoon of the olive oil. When it is hot, add the Jerusalem artichokes, season with salt and sauté for 2–3 minutes until the pieces begin to colour. Transfer the pan to the oven and roast the Jerusalem artichokes for 15–20 minutes until tender.

Do not turn off the oven.

Meanwhile, drain the pearl barley and set aside. Heat a heavy-based saucepan over a medium heat. Add the remaining 1 tablespoon of oil and half the butter. When the butter has melted, add the onions and sauté until they are softened, but not coloured.

Add the pearl barley, stirring until it is well coated in the buttery mixture. Season with salt to taste, then add the wine, increase the heat and leave it to evaporate.

Ladle in enough chicken stock to cover the pearl barley, then stir constantly over a medium heat until it evaporates. Slowly add the remaining stock, ladleful by

Continued on page 170

ladleful, and stirring for a further 20–22 minutes until the barley is tender, but still with a slight bite. Adjust the seasoning with salt and pepper to taste.

Stir the Jerusalem artichokes, remaining butter, Parmesan cheese, cream and parsley into the risotto, then add a splash of sherry vinegar. Cover and keep hot.

Meanwhile, to cook the pheasant breasts, unwrap them from the clingfilm and leave to return to room temperature. Heat a large non-stick, ovenproof sauté or frying pan over a medium-high heat, then add a splash of oil. When it is hot, add the pheasant breasts and fry on both sides so the pancetta sticks to the breasts and crisps slightly. Transfer to the oven and roast for 5–6 minutes until cooked to medium. Be careful not to overcook the breasts. Set aside to rest for 5 minutes, covered with kitchen foil, which will make it easier to cut them.

To serve, cut the breasts into slices and serve with the risotto.

Pot-roasted Pheasant in Mustard Sauce with Dumplings

This heart-warming stew is on the menu at The Scran & Scallie, my Edinburgh pub, every autumn. The combination of pheasant and apple is the perfect match. The dumplings soak up all the juices of the mustard and Calvados sauce, and I love adding a few batons of fresh apple over the top of the dish just before serving for its crunch and freshness.

SERVES 2

---

1 oven-ready pheasant, about 600g

plain flour for dusting

olive oil

80g smoked lardons

2 carrots, peeled and thickly chopped

2 celery sticks, thickly chopped

1 onion, chopped

100ml Calvados

1 litre Chicken Stock (page 279) or Game
 Stock (page 279)

1 bouquet garni

100ml double cream

2 teaspoons wholegrain mustard

sea salt and freshly cracked black pepper

For the dumplings

85g self-raising flour

40g grated suet

15g cooked chestnuts, finely chopped

1½ teaspoons finely chopped parsley

1–2 tablespoons cold water, as needed

To garnish

½ green apple

½ red apple

4 cooked chestnuts, crumbled

chopped flat-leaf parsley

Preheat the oven to 180°C Fan/200°C/Gas Mark 6.

Skin the pheasant, then remove the breasts and legs, separating the thighs. Set aside. (Keep the carcass to make a stock. If you don't want to do that immediately, the bones can be frozen until you're in the mood or have time.)

Season the flour with salt and pepper, then flour the pheasant pieces, shaking off the excess flour.

Heat a large flameproof casserole over a medium-high heat, then add a thin layer of oil. When it is hot, add the pheasant pieces and fry for 4–5 minutes until lightly coloured on both sides. Remove them from the casserole and set aside.

Add the lardons to the casserole and sauté until they render their fat and are coloured all over. Add the carrots, celery and onion to the pan, and continue sautéing them for 2–3 minutes until they are beginning to colour and soften. Pour in the Calvados, stirring to deglaze the casserole, and boil until it reduces by half.

Return the pheasant pieces to the casserole with the chicken stock and bouquet garni, and season with salt and pepper. Return the liquid to the boil. Cover the casserole and place in the oven for 40 minutes.

Meanwhile, make the dumplings. Mix the flour, suet, chestnuts and parsley together. Season with salt and pepper, then stir in just enough water to make a soft dough, as if making pastry. Tip the mixture out onto a lightly floured surface and knead to incorporate the suet. Roll into 4 equal-sized balls. Set aside, covered with a damp cloth, until required.

After the pheasant has cooked for 40 minutes, add the dumplings to the casserole, re-cover the casserole and return it to the oven for a further 35–50 minutes, checking occasionally and adding more stock, if necessary, until the pheasant is tender and the dumplings are puffy.

Continued on page 173

Use a slotted spoon to transfer the meat, vegetables, lardons and dumplings to a tray, cover with kitchen foil and keep hot. Strain the cooking liquid through a chinois or fine sieve, then return it to the washed casserole.

Bring the cooking liquid to the boil and boil until it reduces by one-third. Stir in the cream and mustard and adjust the seasoning with salt and pepper, if necessary. Reduce the heat to medium. Return the pheasant pieces, vegetables, lardons and dumplings to the casserole and warm through, if necessary.

Just before serving, core and cut the apples into matchstick pieces. Serve the pheasant garnished with the apples, chestnuts and parsley.

Pheasant and Partridge Scotch Eggs

This was my late Grandfather Ben's ideal lunch – a good Scotch egg, some strong cheddar and chutney – oh, and let's not forget the good pint of ale. You can easily adapt the recipe depending on what game you can get, but always try to use a good-quality sausage meat to bind it. Personally, I love it when the yolk is a bit soft, but if you like your yolks firmer just cook the egg a little longer.

You need to mince the pheasant and partridge meat for this recipe, I recommend using a mini food processor.

SERVES 4

---

6 free-range eggs

500g good-quality sausage meat

200g pheasant and partridge meat, finely minced

50g cooked chestnuts, crushed

1 tablespoon finely chopped flat-leaf parsley

1 tablespoon wholegrain mustard – I like to use Pommery

80g plain flour, plus extra for flouring your hands

50g pank or dried breadcrumbs

vegetable oil for deep-frying

cheddar cheese – to my mind nothing beats the cheddar from Mull – to serve

tomato chutney, to serve

sea salt and freshly cracked black pepper

The eggs can be soft-boiled, coated and chilled for up to a day before deep-frying and serving. Place 4 eggs in a large saucepan of boiling water, then boil the eggs for 5½ minutes for soft yolks.

In the meantime, place a large bowl of iced water in the sink. As soon as the eggs are cooked, transfer them to the cold water and leave until they are cool enough to handle. Shell the eggs, being careful not to break them, then set aside. (I always cook a few extra just in case some break.)

Place the sausage meat, mixed pheasant and partridge meat, chestnuts, parsley and mustard in to a bowl. Season with salt and pepper and mix well together. Fry a small amount in a well-seasoned pan to taste and adjust the salt and pepper, if necessary.

Beat the remaining eggs in a wide shallow bowl. Place the flour and breadcrumbs in separate wide shallow bowls and season the flour with salt and pepper.

Divide the game mixture into 4 equal-sized portions. Lightly flour your hands and flatten one portion of the sausage mixture into an oval shape in the palm of one hand. Roll one egg in the flour and place it in the middle of the sausage mixture, then gently shape the mixture around the egg, using your fingers to seal any cracks. Lightly roll the sausage-coated egg in the flour, then shake off any excess flour. Add the egg to the beaten egg and roll it around so it is coated, then, finally, roll it in the breadcrumbs, patting them in place. Repeat this stage twice. Repeat with the remaining 3 eggs. At this point you can cover and chill the eggs if not frying straightaway.

When you are ready to fry the eggs, heat enough oil for deep-frying in a deep-fat fryer or heavy-based saucepan until it reaches 160°C, or until a small about of the sausage mixture sizzles or a cube of bread browns in 60 seconds.

Add the eggs and deep-fry for 6–7 minutes until they are golden brown. Use a slotted spoon to remove them from the oil and drain well on kitchen paper. Season with salt and pepper.

Serve the hot Scotch eggs with cheddar cheese, chutney and a little pepper sprinkled over.

Barbecued Beer-can Pheasant

Beer can pheasant! Now, for this recipe I need to give credit to Sean, my Australian chef friend, as it was his genius idea. Pheasant is a great game bird to cook with, but there's a fine line between it being cooked perfectly and over cooked and dry. Cooking the pheasant on top of a can of beer, however, is a really good way of keeping the flesh moist. It's also a really fun process and creates a good vibe for the meal.

I think this is a perfect recipe for a barbecue, especially as now you can buy frames that help support the can and hold it upright during cooking on an unstable surface, as you can see in the picture here.

I never need an excuse to light the barbecue, but if you'd rather cook this in a conventional oven, preheat it to 180°C Fan/200°C/Gas Mark 6. Place the baking tray with the bird on the can in the oven and roast and baste as below until the juices run clear. Set aside to rest covered with kitchen foil for 5 minutes.

SERVES 2

1 oven-ready pheasant, about 600g
2 tablespoons olive oil
1 tablespoon each chopped rosemary
   and thyme leaves
1 can (400ml) of hoppy beer
sea salt and freshly cracked black pepper

Prepare your barbecue so it's ready at a medium heat and the coals are glowing, then position the rack about 20cm above the coals.

Remove the pheasant from the fridge 20 minutes before cooking to bring it up to room temperature.

Using a sharp knife, remove the wishbone from the pheasant. Rub the bird with the olive oil and season well with salt and pepper before sprinkling with the rosemary and thyme.

Open the can of beer and pour out one-quarter of the beer – or drink it! Place the can inside the pheasant's cavity, then place the pheasant on a baking tray to catch all the juices. About three-quarters of the can should fit inside the bird.

Place the baking tray on the grill and leave the pheasant to cook for 25–30 minutes, depending on the size of your bird – I like to baste the pheasant every 5 minutes with the juices that gather in the pan. The pheasant is cooked when you stick a skewer into the thigh and the juices run clear.

Set the pheasant aside to rest for 5 minutes covered with kitchen foil. Taste the juices, adjust the seasoning with salt and pepper, if necessary, then spoon them over the carved bird. This is a simple, rustic dish, so there isn't any reason to strain them first.

Partridge

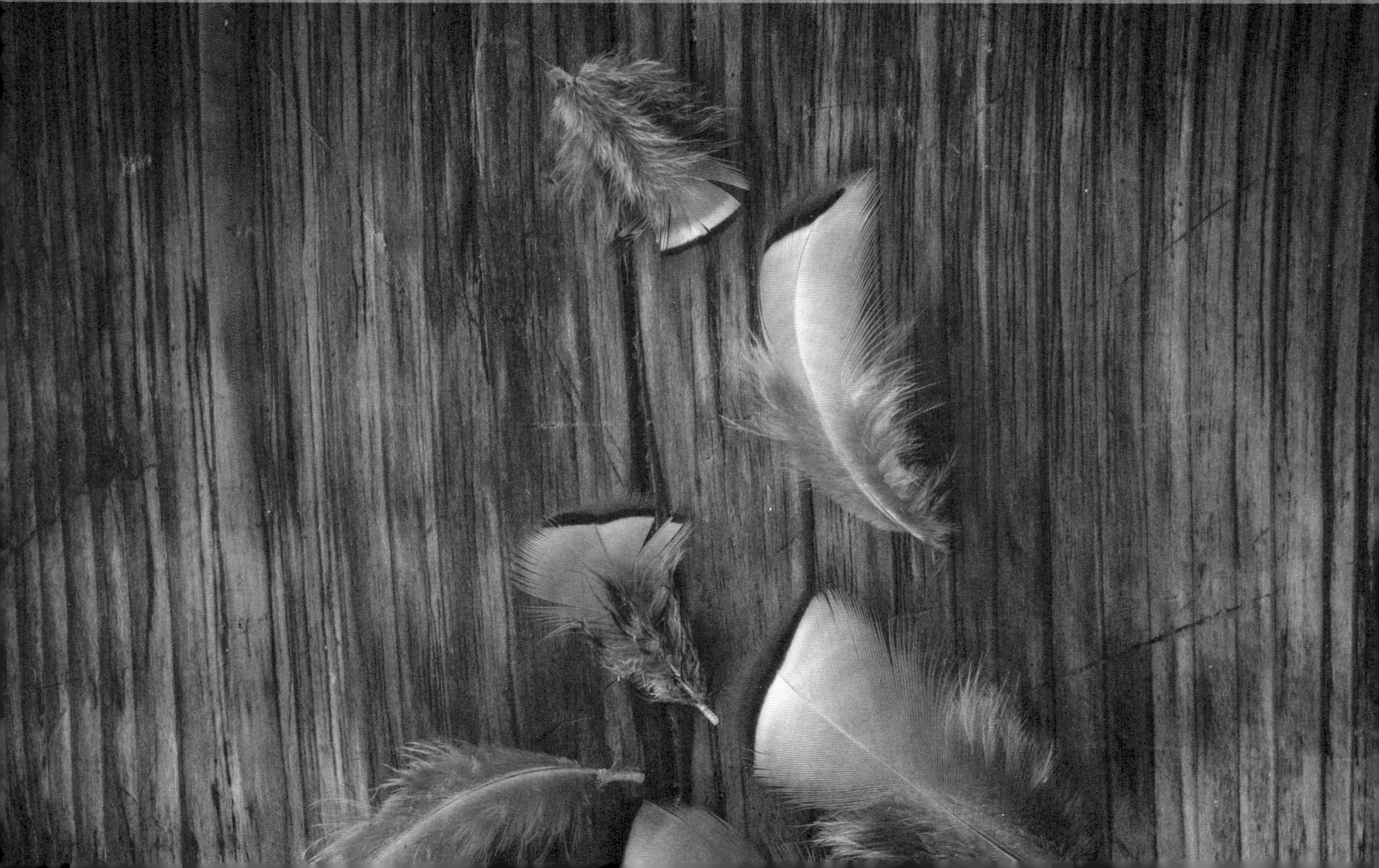

Partridge Breasts and Liver Pâté on Toast

When you start to cook proper seasonal food it is really interesting how dishes naturally come together so all the ingredients complement each other. Everything about this dish screams autumn to me, from the partridge, chicory and apple to the walnuts.

SERVES 4

4 boneless partridge breasts, skinned
olive oil
8 pancetta slices
4 sourdough bread slices
sea salt and freshly cracked black pepper

For the walnut dressing
50g walnuts
1 tablespoon finely chopped shallot
50ml walnut oil
2 teaspoons sherry vinegar

For the liver pâté
20g chicken livers, trimmed
2 partridge livers and 2 partridge hearts, both trimmed – get these from a butcher
5g butter
1 tablespoon finely chopped shallot
1 garlic clove, chopped
1 teaspoon thyme leaves
2 tablespoons brandy
50ml olive oil

For the apple and chicory salad
1 red apple
1 chicory head, trimmed and separated into leaves
½ radicchio head, trimmed and quartered
1 tablespoon chopped flat-leaf parsley

You can make the dressing and pâté in advance, so all you have to do is sear the partridge beasts and mix the salad ingredients together just before serving.

Make the walnut dressing up to 12 hours in advance. Place the walnuts in a non-reactive bowl, reserving a few pieces for sprinkling over the toasts just before serving. Add the shallot, walnut oil and a splash of sherry vinegar to the bowl, and stir together. Season with salt and pepper, then set aside.

To make the liver pâté, very finely chop the chicken and partridge livers and hearts – the finer the better. Heat a well-seasoned sauté or frying pan over a medium-high heat, then add the butter. When it is foaming, add the liver and heart mixture, shallot, garlic and thyme, season with salt and pepper and stir for 1–2 minutes until coloured all over. Add the brandy, stirring to deglaze the pan, and boil until it evaporates. Adjust the seasoning with salt and pepper, if necessary.

Now place the liver mixture in a mortar and use a pestle to mix until puréed, then slowly add the olive oil, mixing as you add it. Taste for seasoning and set aside.

Place a partridge breast between 2 sheets of clingfilm and use a meat mallet or rolling pin to lightly bash until flattened. Repeat with the remaining breasts. Pat all the breasts dry and season them with salt and pepper.

Heat a well-seasoned sauté or frying pan over a medium-high heat, then add a good splash of oil. When it is hot, add the breasts to the pan and sear for 2 minutes on both sides for pink meat in the centre. Set aside to rest for 5 minutes covered with kitchen foil.

While the partridge is resting, add the sliced pancetta to the same pan and fry until crispy, then remove and set aside.

Meanwhile, preheat the grill to high and toast the sourdough bread on both sides. Peel, core and cut the red apple for the salad into wedges.

To serve, spread the liver pâté on the hot toast and add some toasted pancetta to each slice. Top with the partridge breasts and sprinkle with the reserved walnut pieces. Give the dressing a good stir. Combine the apple wedges, chicory and radicchio, and toss with the walnut dressing to serve alongside.

Open Partridge and Pancetta Toasties with Onion Compôte

Who doesn't love a toastie? This open partridge toastie is my way to take the toastie experience to a whole new level. I love to serve it with an onion compôte, which brings a lovely natural sweetness to the dish. Don't be shy to experiment and add other ingredients to give this recipe your own personal touch.

SERVES 4

---

4 partridge breasts, skinned

olive oil

butter for spreading

4 sourdough bread slices

2 hard-boiled free-range eggs, sliced

8 pancetta rashers, cooked until crispy

watercress sprigs

4 slices cheddar cheese – my cheese of choice for this recipe comes from the Isle of Mull, but any strong cheddar would do

sea salt and freshly cracked black pepper

For the onion compôte

50g butter

olive oil

2 white onions, sliced

1 garlic clove, finely chopped

2 teaspoons thyme leaves

The onion compôte is ready to use as soon as it is made, or it can be stored in a covered container in the fridge for up to 3 days. Heat a well-seasoned sauté or frying pan with a lid over a medium-high heat, then add the butter with a splash of oil. When the butter is foaming, add the onions, garlic and thyme and season with salt and pepper. Cover with a wet piece of greaseproof paper, cover the pan with the lid, turn the heat to very low and leave the onions to sweat for 20–25 minutes until they are very tender. Transfer to a plate and set aside to cool.

When you're ready to cook, preheat the grill to high.

Meanwhile, place a partridge breast in between 2 sheets of clingfilm and use a meat mallet or rolling pin to lightly bash until flattened. Repeat with the remaining breasts. Pat the breasts dry and season them all with salt and pepper.

Heat a well-seasoned sauté or frying pan over a medium-high heat, then add a splash of oil. When it's hot, add the breasts and sear them for 2–3 minutes on each side until cooked through, then set aside to rest for 5 minutes covered with kitchen foil. Fry the breasts in batches, if necessary.

Toast the sourdough slices on both sides under the grill, then lightly butter each. Do not turn off the grill.

Spread the pieces of toast with the onion compôte and add the egg slices. Top with the partridge breasts, crispy pancetta, watercress and finally the cheese. Place the toasties under the grill until the cheese melts, then lightly season with salt and cracked pepper.

Grilled Spatchcocked Partridges and White Cabbage

This is a really easy way of cooking partridge, but most importantly it's a very tasty dish. In the photo I've left the feet of partridge on, but you can always remove these if you have trouble fitting them under the grill. I often cook the dish for my young boys, as it makes the meal fun and something a little bit different.

If you have a barbecue, the spatchcocked birds cook well over the coals, too. First light a barbecue and leave the coals until they are glowing and grey. Lightly grease the barbecue rack. Season the partridges and place them skin side down on the rack and grill for 3–4 minutes. It's particularly nice if you can get the skins crispy, but not burnt. Turn the birds over and continue cooking for a further 10–12 minutes until they are tender and the juices run clear if you pierce a thigh, then set aside to rest for 5 minutes, covered with kitchen foil, before serving. While the birds are resting, rub the cabbage wedges with oil and place on the grill rack for about 5 minutes until well coloured.

SERVES 4

4 oven-ready partridges
olive oil
1 large white cabbage head
sea salt and freshly cracked black pepper

For the apple and sultana sauce
1 green apple
olive oil
100g smoked lardons, chopped
50g sultanas
50ml Calvados
100ml Chicken Stock (page 279)
a knob of butter
1 tablespoon very finely chopped chives and chervil
100g seedless red grapes

Soak 8 wooden skewers in cold water for at least 30 minutes before using.

To spatchcock a partridge, place the bird breast side down on a chopping board and cut along both sides of the backbone with kitchen scissors. Turn the bird over and flatten it, pressing down with the palm of your hand. Use kitchen paper to remove any blood from the carcass. Skewer the bird with 2 greased wooden skewers through the legs and body in an X shape. This holds the bird flat, so it cooks more quickly and evenly. Repeat with the remaining birds.

Place the skewered birds in a roasting tray large enough to hold them in a single layer, then drizzle over olive oil, cover the tray with clingfilm and set aside.

Meanwhile, bring a large saucepan of salted water to the boil. Remove the outer leaves from the cabbage, then quarter it, or cut into 8 wedges depending on the size. The secret is to keep the root end attached so the wedges don't fall apart.

Place the wedges in to the boiling water with a plate on top to keep them submerged, turn off the heat and leave for 10-15 minutes until they are tender.

Place a large bowl of iced water in the sink. When the cabbage wedges are tender, use a slotted spoon to immediately transfer the wedges to the iced water to refresh. Remove the wedges from the water and dry with a kitchen cloth, then place them in an ovenproof dish. Cover with olive oil, season with salt and pepper and set aside.

Continued on page 186

To make the salad, peel, core and cut the apple into 5mm dice.

Heat a well-seasoned sauté or frying pan over a medium-high heat, then a good splash of olive oil. When it is hot, add the lardons and sauté until they render their fat and are crispy. Add half the diced apple and all the sultanas and stir for a minute until the apple begins to soften.

Add the Calvados, stirring to deglaze the pan, and boil until it evaporates. Add the chicken stock and boil until it reduces by half. Set aside to finish just before serving.

When you're ready to cook, preheat the grill to high. Place the partridges on the grill rack and grill for 3–4 minutes, then carefully turn them over and grill for a further 10–12 minutes until tender and the juices run clear if you pierce a thigh. Set aside for 5 minutes to rest covered with kitchen foil.

Meanwhile, as soon as the birds are removed from the grill, lightly brush the cabbage wedges with oil and grill for about 5 minutes, turning once halfway through the cooking time, until they are tender and coloured.

Return the sauce to the boil, then stir in the butter. Add the remaining apple, herbs and grapes, and adjust the seasoning with salt and pepper, if necessary.

To serve, place the partridges on the cabbage wedges and spoon over the sauce.

Partridge and Game Pie with Blackberry Compôte

Don't turn the page! This recipe is not as difficult as it looks, and imagine the sense of achievement once you've mastered it. This is a proper traditional game pie, although you can easily twist the recipe depending on what game you can get. It's a real showstopper this one, a real celebration of game.

SERVES 4

15g butter

100g mixed wild mushrooms, such as ceps, girolles and oysters, trimmed, wiped and chopped

2 garlic cloves, chopped

1 white onion, finely chopped

50ml brandy

200g boneless partridge breasts, skinned and coarsely chopped

200g boneless pheasant breasts, skinned and coarsely chopped

200g pork belly in one piece, skinned and coarsely chopped

50g Parma ham in 1 piece, trimmed and coarsely chopped

30ml double cream

1 teaspoon juniper berries, crushed

1 teaspoon freshly grated nutmeg

1½ gelatine leaves

200ml Game Stock (page 279)

Blackberry Compôte (page 85), to serve

sea salt and freshly cracked black pepper

For the hot-water crust pastry

450g plain flour, plus extra for rolling out

2 free-range eggs, beaten, plus 1 extra free-range egg yolk, beaten, to glaze

2 tablespoons thyme leaves

160g lard, diced

200ml water

Allow enough time for the baked pie to cool and chill overnight. The blackberry compôte, which I very much like to serve with this pie, can be made up to 3 days in advance and chilled until required.

To make the pastry, mix the flour, egg, thyme and a pinch of salt together in a large bowl, then make a well in the centre. Melt the lard in the water over a high heat and bring to the boil. Slowly beat the boiling water into the flour mixture, stirring until a ball forms. Wrap in clingfilm and chill for at least 20 minutes.

Heat a large well-seasoned sauté or frying pan over a medium-high heat, then add the butter. When it is foaming, add the mushrooms, garlic and onion and a pinch of salt, and sauté for 2–3 minutes until the onions are softened and the mushrooms are tender. Add the brandy, stirring to deglaze the pan, and boil until all the liquid evaporates. Set aside and leave to cool.

Combine the partridge, pheasant, pork belly and Parma ham in a large bowl. Mix in the cooled onion mixture, making sure all the ingredients are evenly distributed. Use a mincer or a food processor fitted with a mincing blade to coarsely mince the mixture.

Return the minced mixture to the bowl and stir in the cream. Season with the juniper berries, nutmeg and salt and pepper. Fry a small amount in a well-seasoned pan and adjust the salt and pepper, if necessary.

When you are ready to bake the pie, grease the bottom and side of a 20cm round cake tin, at least 6cm deep. Roll out three-quarters of the pastry on a lightly floured work surface with a lightly floured rolling pin until it is about 5mm thick. Use this to line the bottom and side of the tin, gently pressing the pastry into the bottom and leaving an overhang.

Roll out the remaining pastry into a circle large enough to cover the pie, then set aside.

Continued on page 189

Spoon the minced filling into the tin, patting it down to exclude as many air pockets as possible. Lightly brush the rim of the overhanging pastry with water, then place the pastry lid on top and press to seal the join all around. Trim off the excess pastry and crimp the edges together to seal. Reserve the trimmings.

Cut a hole in the centre, about 2.5cm wide. Roll 3 layers of kitchen foil together to make a funnel and insert it in the hole so steam escapes during baking. Roll out a piece of the reserved pastry and use a fluted cutter to cut out a circle about 4cm wide, then use a smaller cutter to cut out a circle the same size as the steam hole. Brush the bottom of the pastry ring with water and place them on top of the pie. Place the pie in fridge to chill for 20 minutes before baking.

Meanwhile, preheat the oven to 180°C Fan/200°C/Gas Mark 6.

Place the pie on a baking sheet and bake for 30 minutes. Lower the oven temperature to 160°C Fan/180°C/Gas Mark 4 and continue baking for a further 1½ hours, or until a metal skewer inserted into the centre feels hot if you press it against your lip. If the pie looks like it is over-browning you can cover the surface with kitchen foil.

Leave the pie to cool completely in the tin on a wire rack.

When the pie is cool, soak the gelatine leaves in a bowl of cold water to cover for 5 minutes, or until softened. Bring the game stock to a simmer and season with salt. Do not allow it to boil.

Remove the gelatine leaves from the water and squeeze out the excess water. Add them to the warm stock, swirling the pan until the gelatine dissolves. Transfer the stock to a large measuring jug.

Very carefully pour one-quarter of the stock through the foil funnel into the pie. Leave the stock to settle for a few seconds, then add another quarter of the stock. Continue this way until you can't pour anymore stock into the pie.

Leave the gelatine to cool completely, then chill the pie in the fridge before cutting. Serve with the blackberry compôte on the side.

Partridges Stuffed with Oats, Orange and Juniper

Oats have always been an integral part of Scottish cooking, so when my Head Chef Lachlan came to me with the idea of stuffing a partridge with oats it made perfect sense. It's really impressive how the oats take on the flavour of the aroma of the partridge to make a really lovely, but original, dish.

— SERVES 4 —

200g porridge oats
100g prunes, finely chopped
1 tablespoon chopped flat-leaf parsley
½ teaspoon ground cinnamon
freshly squeezed juice of 2 oranges
finely grated zest of 1 orange
olive oil
1 tablespoon juniper berries
4 oven-ready partridges
4 pancettta rashers
8 figs, cut in half lengthways
2 long cinnamon sticks, split lengthways
fresh rosemary needles, to garnish
sea salt and freshly cracked black pepper

Preheat the oven to 200°C Fan/220°C/Gas Mark 7.

Put the oats in a bowl, then stir in the prunes, parsley, ground cinnamon, orange juice and zest and a good splash of oil. Crush the juniper berries with a pestle and mortar, then add them to the bowl. Season with salt and pepper and mix well.

To prepare the partridges, use a small knife to cut down either side of a bird's wishbone and remove it. Now use your fingers to check that all the heart and stomach have been removed from the carcass. Repeat with the remaining birds. Divide the oat mixture among the partridge cavities. Cover the back of each bird with a bacon rasher and tie in place with kitchen string, then truss the legs together for even cooking. Season all over with salt and pepper.

Roll any remaining oat mixture into golf ball-sized balls to be cooked alongside the partridges.

Heat a heavy-based roasting tray, or 2 smaller trays, over a medium-high heat, then add a good splash of oil. When it is hot, add the partridges and turn them as necessary until they are coloured all over and the bacon is crispy. Transfer the roasting tray to the oven and roast for 12 minutes, adding any extra oat balls for the final 6 minutes.

Meanwhile, skewer the fig halves with the cinnamon stick pieces, as if making a kebab. Add the figs to the roasting tray and return it to the oven for a further 2–3 minutes until the partridges are medium-rare and the figs are tender. Transfer the birds to a warm plate and set aside to rest for 5 minutes covered with kitchen foil.

While the birds are resting, return the oat balls and figs to the oven.

Serve the partridges straight from the roasting tray, sprinkled with rosemary, with the figs and oat balls too.

Partridge Jellies

When you're having a dinner party and want to impress, this is the perfect wee starter. The great thing, too, is that it's all in the preparation, meaning you won't be stressing about the starter, but instead enjoying your evening. This is a really light refreshing dish, so your guests won't be full after the first course and will still look forward to the next course.

— SERVES 4 —

4 partridge breasts, skinned
600ml Game Stock (page 279)
5 gelatine leaves
4 teaspoons finely chopped tarragon leaves
1 teaspoon finely peeled and chopped fresh ginger
100g leeks, chopped, rinsed, boiled until tender, drained and cooled
100g prunes, stoned
1 carrot, peeled, diced, boiled, drained and cooled
6 quail's eggs, at room temperature
watercress leaves, to garnish
sea salt and freshly cracked black pepper

Bring a large saucepan of water to the boil and set a bowl of iced water in the sink.

While the water is coming to the boil, place a sheet of clingfilm large enough to wrap around a partridge breast horizontally on the work surface, then place a breast on top and roll up tightly to form a sausage shape. Securely knot each end. Repeat with the remaining breasts.

Lower the temperature of the boiling water to a simmer. Add the wrapped breasts and poach for 5 minutes, or until they are firm to the touch. Use a slotted spoon to immediately transfer the breasts to the iced water and leave until cool. Set aside.

Bring 200ml of the game stock just to the simmer – do not boil.

Soak the gelatine in a bowl of cold water to cover for 5 minutes, or until softened, then remove from the water and squeeze out the excess water. Add to the simmering stock, swirling the pan until the gelatine dissolves. Place the remaining stock in a large bowl. Stir the warm stock mixture into the bowl and set aside for about 45 minutes at room temperature.

Three hours before you plan to serve, divide the tarragon, ginger, leek, prunes and carrot among 4 bowls – reserve about one-third of the leek, prunes and carrot to use as a garnish. Pour over enough consommé so each bowl is three-quarters full. Transfer the bowls to the fridge and leave until set.

Meanwhile, to soft-boil the quail's eggs, bring a saucepan of water to the boil. Gently add the eggs and simmer for 2 minutes 25 seconds. Run under cold water until cool enough to handle, then shell and set aside.

Just before you are ready to serve, unwrap the partridge breasts, pat dry and slice about 2.5cm thick. Serve the bowls of jelly with the partridge slices, halved quail's eggs, reserved vegetables and watercress leaves scattered over the tops. Sprinkle with salt and pepper.

Partridge Leg Pastilla with Pickled Red Cabbage

For this recipe I have used the ultra-thin feuilles de brick pastry sheets, available in some supermarkets and North African food shops, but filo pastry would work as well. Remember to always cover the pastry you aren't using with a cloth to stop it from drying out. If you can't get wild girolles mushrooms, cultivated mushrooms would work as well.

— SERVES 8 —

8 partridge legs, patted dry

60g plain flour

olive oil

50g smoked lardons

2 carrots, peeled and finely diced

2 garlic cloves, finely chopped

1 celery stick, finely chopped

50ml brandy

500ml Chicken Stock (page 279)

1 bouquet garni

2 Parma ham slices, finely chopped

50g girolles mushrooms (or oyster or shiitake mushrooms) wiped, trimmed and finely chopped

1 shallot, finely chopped

1 tablespoon finely chopped parsley and tarragon

8 feuilles de brick pastry sheets, about 20 x 20cm, thawed if frozen

20g Clarified Butter (page 276), melted to seal and brush the pastry

vegetable oil for deep-frying

sea salt and freshly crushed black pepper

For the pickled red cabbage

1 red cabbage, cored and thinly sliced

1 red onion, thinly sliced

50ml extra virgin olive oil

2 tablespoons red wine vinegar

balsamic vinegar

1 tablespoon Dijon mustard

1 red apple

100g bramble berries or blackberries

50g walnuts, chopped

20g flat-leaf parsley leaves

The pickled cabbage can be made a day in advance and the partridge legs braised and the pastillas assembled up to 8 hours in advance for deep-frying just before serving.

To make the pickled cabbage, place the red cabbage and onion in a large non-reactive bowl and season with salt and pepper. Add the olive oil, red wine vinegar, a splash of balsamic vinegar and the mustard, and mix together. Set aside until ready to serve.

To make the pastillas, preheat the oven to 180°C Fan/200°C/ Gas Mark 6. Pat the partridge legs dry. Season the flour with salt and pepper, then dust the legs, shaking off any excess.

Heat a large flameproof casserole over a medium-high heat, then add a good splash of oil. When it is hot, add the legs and colour them well all over. Remove them from the pan and set aside.

Add the lardons to the pan and sauté until they render their fat and are coloured all over. Add the carrots, garlic and celery, and continue sautéing for a further 2–3 minutes until the vegetables begin to colour and soften. Add the brandy, stirring to deglaze the pan, and leave it to boil until it evaporates.

Add the stock and bouquet garni and bring to the boil, skimming the surface. Season with salt and pepper. Return the partridge legs to the casserole, cover and place in the oven for 40–45 minutes until the meat is tender enough to flake from the bones.

Remove the legs from the casserole and set aside until cool enough to handle, then pick all the meat off the bones and place in a mixing bowl, discarding the skin and bones. Be careful not to include any small bones.

Meanwhile, strain the cooking liquid into a heavy-based saucepan and discard the flavouring ingredients. Bring the liquid to the boil and reduce by half.

Continued on page 196

Heat a well-seasoned frying pan over a medium-high heat. Add the Parma ham and sauté for 1–2 minutes until crisp. Add the mushrooms, shallot and a pinch of salt, and sauté until the shallot is softened and mushrooms are tender and have re-absorbed the liquid they give off. Stir in the parsley and tarragon, then set aside until completely cool.

When the mushroom mixture is cool, add it to the partridge meat. Add a few spoonfuls of the reduced stock and mix together, so the mixture is slightly loose.

Place 8 large sheets of clingfilm on the work surface. Divide the partridge mixture into 8 equal portions and spread each out into a rectangle 6 x 10cm and about 2.5cm thick, then wrap in the clingfilm and chill for at least 2 hours, or up to 8 hours to set.

Once set, remove the partridge from the clingfilm. Brush one sheet of the pastry with clarified butter and place a partridge portion in the centre. Fold the pastry around and tuck in the ends, then seal the edges with clarified butter. Repeat with all the partridge and pastry. Cover and chill for at least 20 minutes before deep-frying.

Heat enough oil for deep-frying in a deep-fat fryer or heavy-based saucepan until the temperature reaches 180°C, or a cube of bread browns in 30 seconds. Fry the pastillas in batches until the pastry bubbles and is golden brown. Drain well on kitchen paper and keep hot until they are all fried.

Just before serving, finish the pickled red cabbage. Halve and core the red apple, then cut it into thin matchsticks. Add it and the brambles to the red cabbage with the walnuts and parsley, and gently toss everything together, making sure the apples get coated with vinegar and oil so they don't turn brown. Serve the hot pastillas with the cabbage alongside.

Grouse

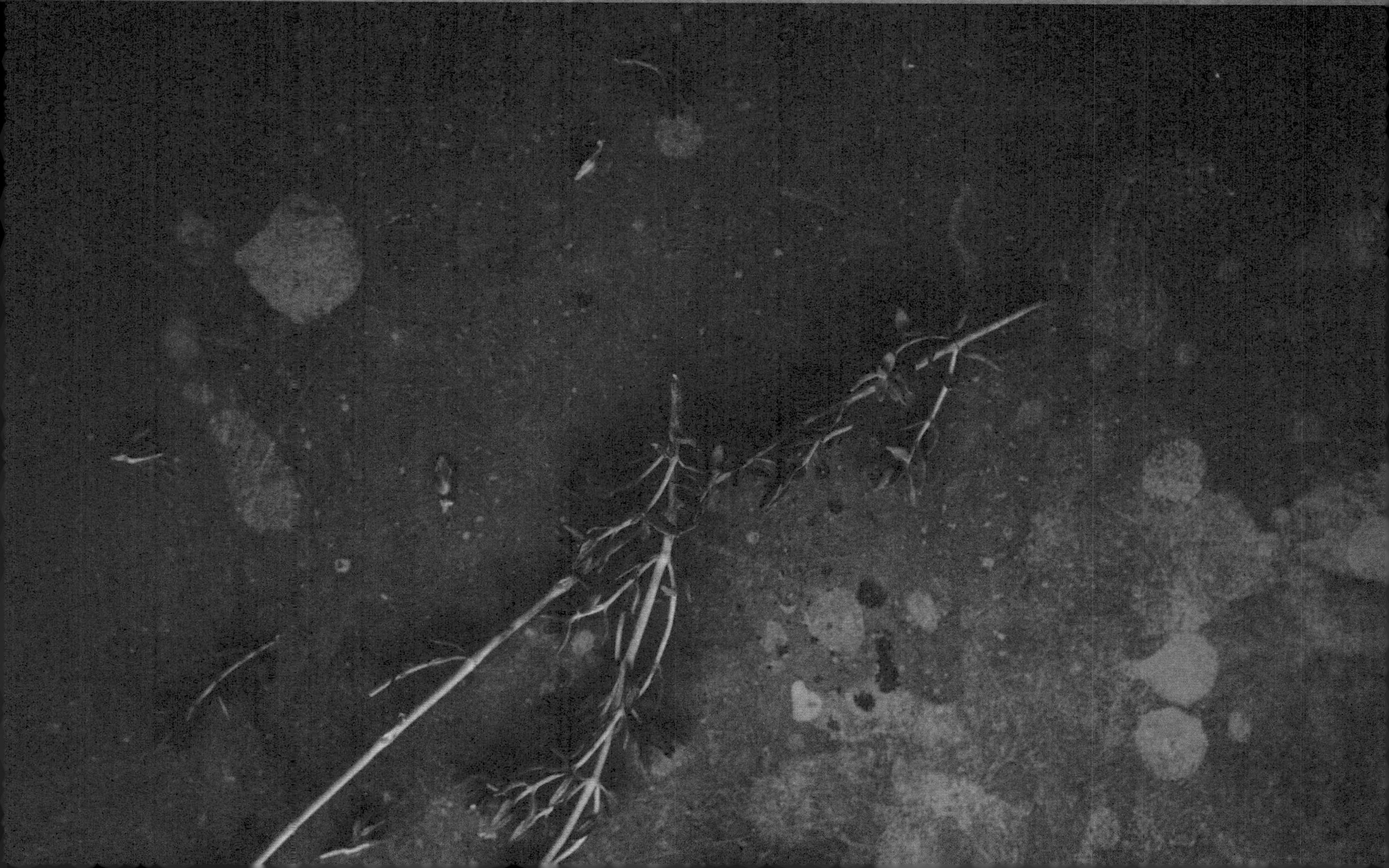

Roasted Grouse Breast and Warm Roast Vegetable Salad

I often make this dish as a starter at home as it's less heavy than eating a whole grouse. I will get all the vegetables cooked before and make the dressing before our guests arrive. That way I've just got to cook the grouse breasts and bring it together for the perfect game starter.

You can buy skinned and toasted hazelnuts from supermarkets, or toast your own. Put the shelled hazelnuts in a large dry sauté or frying pan over a medium-high heat and shake constantly until they are aromatic. Tip them into a tea towel and rub to remove the papery skins, then set aside until required. Watch closely while they are toasting so they don't burn.

SERVES 4

100g carrot

100g celeriac

4 Jerusalem artichokes

4 pumpkin half-moon slices, chopped

olive oil

3 thyme leaves

2 garlic cloves, crushed

2 cooked beetroots

4 young grouse breasts, skinned

15g butter

chopped chives, to garnish

watercress sprigs, to garnish

sea salt and freshly cracked black pepper

For the hazelnut dressing

50g toasted hazelnuts

2 shallots, finely chopped

100ml hazelnut oil

2 teaspoons sherry vinegar

Preheat the oven to 200°C Fan/220°C/Gas Mark 7. Prepare all the vegetables by peeling them and cutting them into wedges about the same size and shape.

Heat a large well-seasoned, ovenproof sauté or frying pan over a medium-high heat, then add a splash of oil. When it is hot, add the carrot, celeriac, Jerusalem artichokes and pumpkin, and sauté for 2–3 minutes until the vegetables are beginning to colour and soften. Add 2 of the thyme sprigs and one of the garlic cloves and season with salt and pepper.

Place the pan in the oven and leave the vegetables to roast for 25–30 minutes, stirring every 10 minutes or so, until they are tender. Test periodically with the tip of a small knife, and remove the vegetable pieces as they are tender. The Jerusalem artichokes will probably take the longest. You want the vegetables to cool at room temperature until they are just warm. Wash and dry the pan, but do not turn off the oven.

Meanwhile, peel the beetroot, wearing plastic gloves to avoid staining your hands, and cut into similar-sized wedges. Add them to the other vegetables for the final 5 minutes to warm through.

To make the dressing, coarsely crush the hazelnuts with a pestle and mortar. Transfer them to a non-reactive bowl with the shallots, hazelnut oil and sherry vinegar, and mix together. Set aside until required.

When you're ready to cook the grouse breasts, pat them dry and season with salt and pepper.

Reheat the pan over a medium-high heat, then add a splash of oil. When it's hot, add the breasts, skin side down, and fry for 2 minutes to colour well, then turn them over and add the remaining thyme sprig and 1 garlic clove and the butter to the pan. When the butter is foaming, spoon it over the breasts.

Place the pan in the oven and roast the breasts for 2 minutes. Set aside to rest for 5 minutes, covered with kitchen foil, before slicing, and then the meat should be pink.

To serve, divide the roasted vegetables and beetroot among 4 plates, then top each with sliced grouse meat. Drizzle over the dressing and garnish with chives and watercress.

Roast Grouse, Game Chips and Bread Sauce

This would be one of my choices for my all-time favourite dishes. Every year at The Kitchin we put the grouse on the menu from the twelfth of August, the Glorious Twelfth, which is the first day of the shooting season. In my opinion, roasting it whole like this and serving it with bread sauce and game chips is, quite simply, the best way to eat grouse.

SERVES 4

4 oven-ready young grouse
4 large pancetta rashers
olive oil
watercress sprigs, to garnish
sea salt and freshly cracked black pepper

For the game chips
4 floury potatoes, such as Maris Piper,
    very thinly sliced, ideally using
    mandolin
vegetable oil for deep-frying

For the bread sauce
1 clove
1 bay leaf
½ onion
400ml milk, plus extra if needed for
    reheating
freshly grated nutmeg, to taste
100g fresh white bread, crusts removed
    and diced
30g butter

The game chips can be made a day in advance and stored in an airtight container until required. After slicing the potatoes, use kitchen paper to pat them dry. Heat enough oil for deep-frying in a deep-fat fryer or a heavy-based saucepan until a potato slice sizzles instantly. Add as many potato slices that fit without over-crowding and fry, stirring constantly, until they are golden brown. Drain well on kitchen paper and sprinkle with salt while they are still hot. Continue until all the slices are fried.

The bread sauce can also be made a day ahead and stored in an airtight container in the fridge for reheating just before serving. Use the clove to secure the bay leaf to the onion half and set aside. Bring the milk to a simmer in a small saucepan, then add the onion and nutmeg. Cover and leave to infuse for 8–10 minutes. Strain the milk into another pan, add the bread and butter and bring to the boil, whisking constantly to break up the bread. Season with salt and pepper and set aside. If not serving immediately, press a piece of clingfilm on the surface to prevent a skin forming.

When you're ready to roast the birds, preheat the oven to 170°C Fan/190°C/ Gas Mark 5. Using a small sharp knife, remove the wishbone from each grouse. Season the cavities with salt and pepper, then cover the breasts of each with 1 folded pancetta rasher. Tie the bacon securely to the birds with kitchen string, then truss the legs for even cooking.

Heat a large well-seasoned, ovenproof sauté or frying pan over a medium-high heat, then add a splash of oil. When it is hot, add the birds and fry until they and the pancetta are nicely coloured all over. Turn the grouse onto one breast, place the pan in the oven and roast for 3 minutes. Turn the birds over onto the other breast and roast for a further 3 minutes. Depending on the size and age of the birds, they may need another minute or 2. If you feel the breasts at the bottom they should have a little spring in them.

Leave the birds to rest for 5 minutes covered with kitchen foil.

Meanwhile, reheat the bread sauce, which might require a little extra milk. Untie the grouse, then serve them garnished with watercress and with the game chips and bread sauce alongside.

Grouse Liver Parfait

At the The Kitchin we have a 'no-waste' policy that means we try to use every part of the animal, which is how this dish came about. The recipe can be easily changed to use pheasant or partridge livers, but always include chicken livers, too, otherwise the parfait might get a bit too strong and gamy.

SERVES 6–8

---

olive oil

100g shallots, finely chopped

100ml port

50ml Madeira

60g butter

60g duck fat

125g grouse livers, trimmed

100g chicken livers, trimmed

6 free-range egg yolks

225ml double cream

50ml brandy

60g Clarified Butter (page 276), melted

blueberries, to garnish

thyme leaves, to garnish

sea salt and freshly cracked black pepper

This rich, creamy mixture will keep for up to 2 weeks in a sealed container in the fridge, but has to be made at least a day before you plan to serve to allow for overnight chilling.

Preheat the oven to 90°C Fan/110°C/Gas Mark ¼.

Meanwhile, heat a well-seasoned sauté or frying pan over a medium-high heat, then add a splash of oil. When it is hot, add the shallots and sauté for 2–3 minutes until softened, but not coloured. Add the port and Madeira, stirring to deglaze the pan, and boil until a syrupy consistency forms. Transfer the shallot reduction to a food processor and set aside.

Melt the butter and duck fat together in the same pan, then add to the shallot reduction in the food processor with the grouse livers, chicken livers, egg yolks and cream. Season with salt and pepper, then add the brandy and process until blended. Pass through a fine sieve to ensure the parfait mix has a smooth consistency.

Transfer the mixture to 2 or 3 small preserving jars and seal. Place the jar in a roasting tray and pour in enough boiling water to come half way up the sides, then place the tray in the oven for 1 hour. Remove the parfaits from the water bath and leave to cool completely, then place in the fridge overnight.

The following day, scrape off any brown skin that might have formed. Pour the clarified butter over, add a few blueberries and thyme leaves and leave to cool, then re-seal and chill until required.

The Ultimate 11s Grouse Sandwiches

When on a grouse shoot, 11am is traditionally the time you stop for a break and refuel your energy when out on the moors. This grouse sandwich is perfect for elevenses, but also tastes amazing at home. Don't be shy of trying this recipe with partridge.

SERVES 4

---

4 young grouse breasts, skinned

60g plain flour

6 free-range eggs

1 tablespoon milk

100g panko or dried breadcrumbs

vegetable oil

8 black pudding slices

4 large sourdough bread slices

butter for spreading

watercress sprigs, to serve

sea salt and freshly cracked black pepper

For the watercress mayonnaise

100g Mayonnaise (page 276)

100g watercress sprigs, rinsed and
   trimmed

1 teaspoon freshly squeezed lemon
   juice, or to taste

First make the watercress mayonnaise, which will keep in a covered container in the fridge for up to 7 days. Place the mayonnaise and watercress in a blender or food processor and blend with the pulse setting until it is smooth and green. Add the lemon juice and salt and pepper, then cover and chill until required.

Place a grouse breast between 2 sheets of clingfilm and use a meat mallet or rolling pin to lightly bash until flattened. Repeat with the remaining breasts and pat them dry.

Just before you're ready to cook, place the flour in a shallow bowl and season with salt and pepper. Beat 2 of the eggs with the milk in another shallow bowl, and place the breadcrumbs in a third shallow bowl. One by one, dip the breasts in the flour to cover completely, patting off the excess, then dip them in the eggs and finally in the breadcrumbs, patting the crumbs on well.

Heat a large well-seasoned sauté or frying pan over a medium-high heat, then add about a 5mm layer of oil. When it's hot, add the breasts and fry for 2–3 minutes on each side until golden brown and crispy. Cook them in batches, if necessary. As each fillet is cooked, transfer it to kitchen paper to drain well.

Wipe out the pan, then return it to the heat and add a small amount more oil. Add the black pudding and fry for 3 minutes, turning once, or until cooked through and slightly crusty. Set aside and keep hot.

Wipe out the pan again, then return it to the heat. Add just enough oil to thinly cover the surface and when it's hot, crack in the 4 remaining eggs and fry until cooked as you desire.

Meanwhile, toast the sourdough bread.

To assemble, butter the hot toast, then spread with watercress mayonnaise. Add the grouse, then the black pudding, lots of watercress leaves and finally a fried egg with freshly cracked black pepper sprinkled over the tops. Serve the remaining watercress mayonnaise on the side.

Poached Grouse Breast and Spelt Autumn Salad

With more and more people enjoying healthy grains this is the perfect dish to fill you up, but making sure you still get that magical flavour of autumn. You can make the salad with any other game bird or poultry, but grouse is my first pick. And, always try to get young grouse for this, as they are the most tender.

SERVES 2

200g spelt

olive oil

100g wild mushrooms, such as girolles, wiped and trimmed

400ml Chicken Stock (page 279)

1 garlic clove, crushed

1 thyme sprig

2 young grouse breasts, skin on

100g celeriac

1 red apple

½ pear

100g blueberries

2 celery stalks with leaves, finely chopped

1 carrot, peeled and cut into fine matchsticks

2 teaspoons finely chopped shallot

50g walnuts, chopped, to serve

sea salt and freshly cracked black pepper

For the apple dressing

2 teaspoons honey

2 teaspoons Dijon mustard

2 teaspoons finely chopped shallot

1½ teaspoons cider vinegar

sherry vinegar

150ml olive oil

150ml vegetable oil

1 green apple

2 teaspoons chopped chives

Rinse the spelt well under cold running water, then leave it to soak for ideally 24 hours in cold water to cover, but at least 1–2 hours.

When you're ready to cook it, bring a large saucepan of salted water to the boil. Drain the spelt and rinse, then add it to the boiling water and boil for 40–45 minutes until tender, but still holding its shape. Drain well and set aside to cool completely.

Heat a small well-seasoned sauté or frying pan over a medium-high heat, then add a splash of oil. When it is hot, add the mushrooms with a pinch of salt and sauté until they are tender and have absorbed the liquid they give off. Set aside and leave to cool.

For the dressing, whisk the honey, mustard, shallot, cider vinegar and a splash of sherry vinegar together in a large non-reactive bowl, whisking until an emulsion forms. Slowly add the olive and vegetable oils, whisking constantly, until a thick dressing forms. If it's too thick, stir in a little hot water. Season with salt and pepper, then halve, core and finely dice the apple. Stir in the apple and chives, then set aside.

Heat the stock in a heavy-based saucepan until it is 'smoking', or almost boiling, then season lightly with salt. Add the garlic and thyme and simmer for 2 minutes to infuse.

Add the grouse breasts and poach over a medium heat for 6–8 minutes. Turn off the heat and leave the breasts to cool in the stock for a further 5–7 minutes. Meanwhile, just before you're ready to serve, peel, halve, core and cut the celeriac into fine matchsticks and stir into the dressing to prevent discolouration. Halve, core and cut the red apple into fine matchsticks, and core and cut the pear into thin matchsticks, adding both to the dressing as they are prepared.

Add the spelt, sautéed mushrooms, blueberries, celery stalks with their leaves, carrot and shallot to the bowl. Carefully shred the breast meat, discarding the skin, then add it to the salad with the walnuts. Adjust the seasoning with salt and pepper and toss everything together.

Braised Grouse with Autumn Dumplings

There is nothing better in the autumn or winter than a lovely braised grouse stew. Braising the grouse is a great way to use the older grouse, which are cheaper to buy than the young birds. It's the slow gentle cooking that makes the flesh tender. I love how the dumplings soak up all the flavour in this dish.

—————— SERVES 4 ——————

4 boneless grouse breasts, quartered

50g plain flour

vegetable oil

100g smoked lardons

2 carrots, peeled and cut into 2cm dice

2 garlic cloves, chopped

1 onion, chopped

150g button mushrooms, trimmed, wiped and thickly chopped

1 bay leaf

1 bouquet garni

100ml brandy

1 litre Game Stock (page 279) or Grouse Stock (page 212)

50g whole cooked chestnuts, drained if necessary

chopped fresh parsley, to garnish

sea salt and freshly cracked black pepper

For the autumn dumplings (makes 12)

125g plain flour

½ teaspoon baking powder

a large pinch of fine table salt

60g grated suet

4 teaspoons chopped cooked chestnut

30g peeled pumpkin, very finely chopped

1 teaspoon thyme leaves

4–5 tablespoons cold water

Preheat the oven to 180°C Fan/200°C/Gas Mark 6. Pat the grouse pieces dry. Season the flour with salt and pepper, then dust the grouse pieces with the flour, shaking off the excess.

Heat a large flameproof casserole over a medium-high heat, then add a splash of oil. When it is hot, add the grouse pieces and colour well on both sides, then remove them from the casserole and set aside. You will need to cook the grouse in batches.

Return the casserole to the heat, add the lardons and sauté until they render their fat and are coloured. Add the carrots, garlic and onion, and continue sautéing for a further 2–3 minutes until they are beginning to colour and soften. Add the mushrooms, bay leaf and bouquet garni with a pinch of salt, then sauté for a further 2–3 minutes until the mushrooms give off their liquid.

Add the brandy, stirring to deglaze the casserole, and boil until it evaporates. Return the grouse pieces to the cassserole, pour in the stock and season with salt and pepper, then bring to the boil. Cover the casserole and transfer it to the oven.

After the casserole has been in the oven for 45 minutes, make the dumplings. Sift the flour, baking powder and salt together in a large bowl, then stir in the suet. Add the chopped chestnuts, pumpkin and thyme, and mix together, making a well in the centre. Add the water and mix until a sticky dough forms. Lightly flour your hands and shape the dough in Brussels sprout-sized balls.

Add the dumplings and whole chestnuts to the casserole, re-cover and return to the oven for a further 10 minutes, or until the meat is tender and the dumplings are puffy and cooked through. Adjust the seasoning with salt and pepper, if necessary. Serve sprinkled with chopped parsley.

Grouse and Girolle Broth with Mushroom and Liver Toasts

People are always asking me what to do with the poor older grouse, which are never as tender as the young birds. I usually suggest making a broth, as the meat will be beautifully tender after simmering in the soup. I often make a big batch of this soup to freeze, ready to enjoy through winter.

Grouse hearts can replace the livers in the topping for the toasts. You need two well-trimmed and finely chopped hearts if you don't want to use the livers.

--- SERVES 4 ---

vegetable oil
50g smoked lardons
1 carrot, peeled and finely diced
50g celery, finely chopped
1 onion, finely chopped
50g leeks, trimmed, finely chopped and
   rinsed
120g pearl barley
150g girolle mushrooms, trimmed and
   wiped
50g cooked chestnuts, drained if
   necessary and sliced
chopped parsley, to garnish
sea salt and freshly cracked black pepper

**For the grouse stock (makes about 1
   litre)**
2 oven-ready grouse (old or young), with
   the livers (or hearts) reserved
2 garlic cloves, crushed
1 carrot, peeled and roughly chopped
1 celery stick, roughly chopped
½ onion, roughly chopped
1 bouquet garni

For the mushroom and liver toasts
4 reserved grouse livers
olive oil
4 Parma ham slices, finely chopped
1 teaspoon finely chopped shallots
200g girolle mushrooms, trimmed, wiped
   and finely chopped
4 teaspoons chopped parsley
4 sourdough bread slices

First make the grouse stock, which will keep in a covered container in the fridge for up to 3 days, or in the freezer for up to 3 months. Place the grouse into a large stockpot and cover with 2.5 litres of cold water and bring to the boil, skimming the surface, as necessary. As soon as the water boils, turn the heat down to a simmer and add the garlic, carrot, celery, onion and the bouquet garni. Season with salt and pepper and leave the grouse to simmer for 30 minutes.

Remove the birds from the pot, carefully cut off the breasts and set aside. Return the carcasses to the pot and continue simmering, partially covered, for a further 1½–2 hours to make the rich stock. Strain the stock through a chinois or fine sieve, reserving at least 1 litre and discarding the flavouring ingredients. When the carcasses are cool enough to handle, remove the meat and finely chop along with the breasts. Set aside.

Heat a large saucepan over a medium-high heat, then add a splash of oil. When it is hot, add the lardons and sauté until they render their fat and are well coloured. Add the finely chopped carrot, celery, onion and leeks and the barley, and continue sautéing for 2–3 minutes until the vegetables are starting to colour and soften. Add the reserved stock. Season lightly with salt and pepper and bring to the boil, then reduce the heat and simmer for 40–45 minutes until all the vegetables are tender.

Meanwhile, heat a small well-seasoned sauté or frying pan over a medium-high heat. Add the 150g girolle mushrooms with a pinch of salt and sauté until they are tender and have absorbed the liquid they give off. Remove from the pan and set aside to add to the broth just before serving.

To make the mixture for the toast, use a sharp knife to trim and cut the livers into small pieces and set aside.

Heat a well-seasoned sauté or frying pan over a high heat, then add a splash of oil. When it is hot, add the Parma ham and cook quickly. Add the livers and season with salt and pepper, then sauté for 1 minute. Remove from the pan and set aside.

Return the pan to the heat and add a little more oil. Add the shallots and girolles and season with salt and pepper – as the liquid comes off the mushrooms you can carefully spoon this into the soup – and sauté until they are tender. Set aside and keep hot.

Return the livers to the pan with the parsley and mix together. Just before you are ready to serve, toast the sourdough bread.

To serve, add the grouse meat and chestnuts to the broth, and adjust the seasoning, if necessary. Spread the liver mixture on the toast. Add the sautéed mushrooms to the broth, sprinkle with parsley and serve.

Grouse Sausage Rolls

I don't know anyone who doesn't enjoy a sausage roll, but this is really a great and easy way to make it even better by adding grouse to the filling. I've noticed this is also a really popular dish with the kids. It's really important you buy good-quality sausage meat to mix with the grouse. These are great with the red cabbage salad (see page 194).

SERVES 8

200g young grouse breasts, skinned and finely chopped

200g sausage meat

vegetable oil

30g wild mushrooms, such girolles, ceps or oysters, trimmed and wiped

50g Parma ham, finely chopped

2 tablespoons finely chopped shallots

2 tablespoons finely chopped cooked chestnuts

1 tablespoon peeled and finely diced quince

1 teaspoon thyme leaves

400g puff pastry, thawed if frozen

plain flour for dusting and rolling

1 free-range egg yolk, beaten

watercress sprigs, to serve (optional)

1 green apple, to serve (optional)

sea salt and freshly cracked black pepper

The sausage rolls can be assembled up to one day before baking, but if you do that don't brush the surface with the egg wash until just before they go in the oven.

Mix the grouse meat and sausage meat together in a bowl, then set aside.

Heat a well-seasoned sauté or frying pan over a medium-high heat, then add a splash of oil. When it is hot, add the mushrooms with a pinch of salt and sauté until they are tender and have absorbed the liquid they give off. Tip them out of the pan and finely chop. When they are cool, add to the bowl with the grouse meat.

Heat a little more oil in the same pan over a high heat. Add the Parma ham and sauté for 1 minute. Add the shallots, chestnuts, quince and thyme, and season with salt and pepper. Sauté everything together, then set aside to cool.

Once the ingredients have cooled, add them to the meats and mix well by hand. Fry a small amount in a well-seasoned pan to taste and adjust the salt and pepper, if necessary.

Roll out the puff pastry on a lightly floured work surface with a lightly floured rolling pin into a 40 x 30cm rectangle, then transfer it to a floured baking sheet that will fit in your fridge. Lightly flour your hands and shape the sausage meat mixture into a long, even roll, then place along one long side of the pastry, about 1cm from the edge. Brush the edges with egg, then gently lift the remaining pastry over the sausage roll and press the edges together, using the floured tines of a fork to seal. Transfer to the fridge for at least 20 minutes before baking.

Meanwhile, preheat the oven to 200°C Fan/220°C/Gas Mark 7 and line a baking sheet with greaseproof paper.

Brush the long roll with the egg wash, then cut into 8 equal portions and place them on the baking sheet. Bake for 30 minutes, or until the pastry is golden brown. Serve hot or at room temperature. I particularly like these with a watercress and apple salad, and they go well with pickled red cabbage.

Roast Pigeon and Cherry Sauce

Sometimes we chefs forget how difficult it is to make sauces at home. In our restaurants, of course, we have access to all the lovely stocks and sauces. However, this sauce is restaurant quality but easy to make at home. It is a great sauce to go with the pigeon and cherries work incredibly well with the mild gamy flavour of the pigeon. If you can't get hold of fresh cherries, marinated ones work fine, too.

SERVES 4

4 oven-ready wood pigeons, with the wishbones removed

4 garlic cloves, peeled but left whole

4 rosemary sprigs

4 thyme sprigs

olive oil

100g butter, plus an extra knob for finishing

200ml full-bodied red wine

50ml port or kirsch

350ml Game Stock (page 279) or Chicken Stock (page 279)

200g cherries, stoned

300g Wilted Spinach (page 276), hot, to serve

sea salt and freshly cracked black pepper

Preheat the oven to 200°C Fan/220°C/Gas Mark 7. Season the pigeons all over and in the cavities with salt and pepper, then divide the garlic, rosemary and thyme among the cavities. Truss the legs together with kitchen string.

Heat 2 large well-seasoned, ovenproof sauté or frying pans over a medium-high heat, then add a good splash of olive oil. When it is hot, add the pigeons and colour all over for 3 minutes. Add the butter and when it is foaming, baste the birds.

Transfer the pans to the oven and roast the pigeons for 6 minutes, which should give you pink meat. Remove the pans from the oven, un-truss the birds and tip the juices from all the cavities into one of the pans, then set the birds aside to rest, covered with kitchen foil, while you finish the recipe.

Remove the excess fat from the pan, then return it to the heat. Add the wine and port, stirring to deglaze the pan, and boil until the liquid evaporates. Add the game stock and continue boiling to reduce it by half, then stir in the cherries. Reduce the heat and simmer until they are soft. Swirl in the knob of butter, then adjust the seasoning with salt and pepper, if necessary.

Serve the roasted pigeons with cherry sauce and the wilted spinach alongside.

Smoked Pigeon and Poached Egg Salad

Smoked pigeon is a great ingredient that makes a satisfying salad very quickly and easily. I always like it when a salad is an adventure of flavours and textures, which is what you get with this one.

—————————————— SERVES 4 ——————————————

olive oil

4 Bayonne ham slices

50g Clarified Butter (page 276)

3 thick slices sourdough bread, cut into 20 bite-size chunks

10 frizzy salad leaves, such as frissé

½ head of oak leaf lettuce

small bunch watercress leaves

sherry vinegar

4 free-range eggs, at room temperature

4 smoked pigeon breasts, skinned and sliced

100g cherry tomatoes, halved

2 shallots, sliced

4 tablespoons pine nuts

4 tablespoons cooked sweetcorn

sea salt and coarsely cracked black pepper

For the vinaigrette

1 teaspoon Dijon mustard

50ml balsamic vinegar

250ml vegetable oil

50ml extra virgin olive oil

You can prepare most of the components of this salad in advance so all you have to do is poach the eggs and assemble the salad just before serving.

The vinaigrette will keep for up to 3 days in a covered container in the fridge. Place the mustard in a non-reactive bowl with the vinegar and whisk until an emulsion forms. Slowly whisk in the vegetable oil, followed by the olive oil, then season with salt and pepper. If the dressing is too thick, add a little hot water.

The crispy bacon and croûtons can be fried several hours in advance. Heat a well-seasoned sauté or frying pan over a medium-high heat, then add a little oil. When it is hot, add the Bayonne ham slices and cook on each side until crisp. Leave to drain on a plate lined with kitchen paper.

To make the croûtons, melt the clarified butter with any fat remaining in the same pan. When it is foaming, add the bread cubes and stir them around for 3–4 minutes until they are golden brown and crispy. Tip them onto the kitchen paper to drain as well, then set aside until required.

Rinse all the salad leaves well, then pat dry. Cover and chill until you're ready to assemble the salad.

Poach the eggs just before you plan to serve so they are hot. Bring a large saucepan of water to the boil, add a splash of vinegar and reduce the heat until bubbles just break the surface. One by one, break an egg into a small bowl, then whisk the water to create a whirlpool effect, and gently drop in the egg. When they are all in the water, poach for 3 minutes, which will cook them, but keep the yolks soft. Use a slotted spoon to transfer the eggs to kitchen paper to drain, and keep hot.

To assemble the salads, divide the salad leaves among 4 plates. Arrange the sliced pigeon on top of each, then sprinkle over the croûtons, cherry tomatoes, shallots, pine nuts and sweetcorn, and break the crispy bacon into large pieces as you add it. Add a poached egg to each, then drizzle with vinaigrette, sprinkle with black pepper and serve.

Pigeon, Grape and Caramelised Walnut Salad

Cooking the pigeon nice and pink is really important, but it's also equally important to cook the French beans properly. For me, many people either under-cook or over-cook French beans, and to get them just perfectly cooked is a skill – they should just be tender. The caramelised walnuts are a great garnish to keep in your fridge, as they can easily bring many dishes to life.

4 wood pigeon breasts, skinned
olive oil
50g butter
sea salt and freshly cracked black pepper

For the caramelised walnuts
1 tablespoon clear honey
2 teaspoons soft light brown sugar
10g butter
75g shelled walnuts halves

For the pigeon liver dressing
4 pigeon livers, trimmed and cleaned
olive oil
1 tablespoon finely chopped shallot
1 tablespoon sherry vinegar
50ml walnut oil

For the salad
200g French beans, trimmed
200g lamb's lettuce, rinsed and dried
handful chervil and parsley leaves
1 shallot, sliced
4 celery hearts
50g seedless red grapes, halved

You can prepare most of the components of this salad in advance, so all you have to do assemble it just before serving.

The caramelised walnuts can be made up to 3 days in advance and stored in the fridge until required. Preheat the oven to 170°C Fan/190°C/Gas Mark 5 and line a baking sheet with greaseproof paper. Melt the honey, sugar and butter with a pinch of salt in a small heavy-based saucepan over a low heat, then stir in the nuts. Spread out the nuts on the baking sheet and bake for 10–12 minutes, stirring every 2 minutes, until caramelised. Transfer to a plate to cool, then store in an airtight container in the fridge (you can use any leftovers to bring any dish to life).

The liver dressing can be made a couple of hours in advance and chilled until about 15 minutes before required so it returns to room temperature. Pat the livers dry and season them with salt and pepper. Heat a well-seasoned sauté or frying pan over a medium-high heat, then add a splash of oil. When it is hot, add the livers and fry or 1–2 minutes until they are pink throughout, then set aside.

Add the shallot to the oil remaining in the pan and sauté for 1 minute, or until it is softened. Add the sherry vinegar, stirring to deglaze the pan, and boil until it evaporates. Tip the mixture into a blender, add the pigeon livers and blend everything together. With the motor running, slowly add the walnut oil through the feed tube. If the dressing is too thick, add a little hot water, so the consistency is like a vinaigrette. Adjust the seasoning with salt and pepper, if necessary, and set aside.

To cook the French beans for the salad, bring a large saucepan of salted water to the boil and put a bowl of iced water in the sink. Add the beans to the pan and boil until they are just tender. Drain well and immediately transfer to the iced water to stop the cooking and set the colour, then set aside.

Continued on page 224

Cook the pigeon breasts just before you plan to assemble the salad so they are still hot when you serve. Preheat the oven to 170°C Fan/190°C/Gas Mark 5. Pat the breasts dry and season them with salt and pepper.

Heat a large well-seasoned, ovenproof sauté or frying pan over a medium-high heat, then add a good splash of oil. When it is hot, add the breasts to the pan and brown them for 2 minutes on each side. Add the butter, and when it is foaming, baste the breasts.

Transfer the pan to the oven and roast the breasts for 3 minutes for pink meat. Set aside to rest for 5 minutes covered with kitchen foil.

Meanwhile, assemble the salad. Drain the French beans and pat dry. Place the beans, lamb's lettuce, chervil and parsely leaves and shallot rings in a bowl and toss together, then season with a little salt and divide among 4 plates. Thickly slice the pigeon breasts and add to the salad, then drizzle with the liver dressing and any accumulated juices from while the birds were resting and season again, if necessary. Add the celery hearts, sprinkle with the caramelised walnuts and grapes and serve immediately.

Wood Pigeon Breasts with Creamed Mushrooms in Vol-au-vents

Trust me, vol-au-vents are back in fashion and I totally see why. They make for the perfect starter and can easily be prepared in advance. They also look great. I love to use fresh peas and broad beans when they're in season and depending on how cheffy you want to be, you can peel the broad beans like I have done for the photograph – they look so fresh and appetizing, don't you think? To do this, blanch the beans in boiling water, the drain them well and rinse under cold water to stop the cooking and set the colour. Then just use your fingers to peel off the thick grey outer skin. Add them to the pan when the peas are tender and heat through.

SERVES 6

---

2 wood pigeon breasts
2 tablespoons olive oil
sea salt and freshly cracked black pepper

For the vol-au vents
250g puff pastry, thawed if frozen
plain flour for rolling out
1 free-range egg yolk, beaten

For the creamed mushrooms
a knob of butter
2 tablespoons olive oil
60g smoked lardons
200g button mushrooms, trimmed, wiped
    and chopped
100ml double cream
50g shelled peas and broad beans,
    thawed if frozen
2 teaspoons wholegrain mustard – I use
    Pommery

First make the vol-au-vents, which can be prepared up to 2 days in advance and stored in an airtight container until required, or frozen for up to 1 month and reheated from frozen.

Roll out the puff pastry on a very lightly floured surface with a lightly floured rolling pin until it is 4mm thick. Use a 9cm fluted round cutter to cut out 12 circles. Use a 6cm round cutter to cut the centre out of 6 of the circles. Chill the pastry circles for at least 20 minutes.

Meanwhile, preheat the oven to 200°C Fan/220°C/Gas Mark 7.

Place the 6 whole circles on a baking sheet and brush with beaten egg yolk. Place the remaining pastry rings on top and brush the tops with a little beaten egg – be careful not to let the egg drip down the sides. Bake for 15 minutes, or until the pastry is well risen and golden brown. Use a small spoon to remove the pastry in the centre, leaving a crisp shell for filling. Leave to cool completely on a wire rack, then store until required.

To make the creamed mushrooms, heat a large well-seasoned sauté or frying pan over a medium heat, then melt the butter with the oil. When they are hot, add the lardons and sauté until they have rendered their fat and are coloured all over. Add the mushrooms with a pinch of salt and continue sautéing until they are tender and have absorbed the liquid they give off.

Stir in the cream and bring to the boil. Stir in the peas, beans and mustard, and simmer until the peas and beans are tender. Adjust the seasoning with salt and pepper. Set aside and keep hot.

When you are ready to cook, heat the oven to 170°C Fan/190°C/Gas Mark 5. Season the pigeon breasts all over with salt and pepper.

Continued on page 227

Heat a large well-seasoned, ovenproof sauté or frying pan over a medium-high heat, then add the oil. When it is hot, add the breasts to the pan and brown them for 2 minutes on both sides. Transfer the pan to the oven and roast the breasts, skin side up, for 3 minutes for pink meat. Set aside to rest for 5 minutes covered with kitchen foil.

When the breasts come out of the oven, turn the temperature up to 200°C Fan/220°C/Gas Mark 7.

Meanwhile, reheat the mushroom mixture and reheat the vol-au-vents in the oven for 1–2 minutes, if necessary. Remove the skin from the pigeon breasts and finely chop the flesh. Stir the chopped flesh and any cooking juices into the mushroom mixture.

Divide the mushroom mixture among the vol-au-vents and serve.

Pigeon with Garlic and Rosemary Fondant Potatoes

Wood pigeon is readily available and offers very good value, as it's such a versatile product. Whenever you cook meat on the bone it's always that little bit juicier, in my opinion. Don't be scared to try the offal sauce – it works really well with the full-flavoured pigeon meat and fondant potatoes.

SERVES 4 VERY HUNGRY DINERS

4 wood pigeon crowns – get these from a
    butcher or game dealer
4 pigeon hearts and 4 pigeon livers
25g butter
4 teaspoons finely chopped shallots
1 tablespoon brandy
100ml Beef Stock (page 278)
red wine vinegar
olive oil
rosemary sprigs, to garnish
sea salt and freshly cracked black pepper

**For the garlic and rosemary fondant
    potatoes**
20 small baby potatoes, well scrubbed
    with a nail brush and halved
100g butter, diced
4 garlic cloves, lightly crushed
a small handful rosemary needles

Ask your butcher to prepare the pigeons for you, reserving the heart and liver from each. Have the legs and under bone cut off from each bird, leaving the crowns. Rub the crowns with olive oil, season with salt and pepper and set aside while you make the potatoes and sauce.

To make the fondant potatoes, place the potatoes cut side down in a large well-seasoned sauté or frying pan. Pour in enough cold water to come just to the top of the potatoes. Add the butter, garlic and rosemary, and season with salt. Cover the pan tightly with kitchen foil and place it over a high heat. When the water boils, turn the heat down slightly and leave the liquid to be absorbed until the pan is dry – it is very important that you don't shake the pan while the liquid reduces. The butter will start to colour – don't worry and let it colour for 1–2 minutes, then remove the pan from the heat and leave the potatoes to cool. Just don't shake it! Once cool, turn the potatoes, which should be beautifully golden and full of flavour.

Meanwhile, preheat the oven to 180°C Fan/200°C/Gas Mark 6.

To make the sauce, very finely chop the hearts and livers – the finer the better. Heat another well-seasoned sauté or frying pan over a medium-high heat, then add the butter. When it is foaming, add the hearts, livers and shallots, season with salt and pepper and stir for 1–2 minutes until the shallots soften. Add the brandy, stirring to deglaze the pan, and boil until it evaporates. Add the stock and continue boiling until it reduces by half. Add a splash of vinegar and adjust the seasoning, if necessary. Set aside and keep hot.

To cook the pigeon *a la plancha*, you need a large, flat griddle, or you can use a large well-seasoned sauté or frying pan. Heat the griddle or pan over a medium-high heat, then add just a splash of oil. When it is hot, add the crowns and fry them for 6–8 minutes until they are well coloured all over. They will be brown, but the flesh should remain pink. Set aside to rest for 5 minutes covered with kitchen foil.

Meanwhile, place the potatoes in to the oven for reheating for 5 minutes while the birds are resting. Re-heat the sauce, if necessary. Serve the pigeon crowns with the sauce spooned over and with the potatoes alongside, garnished with the rosemary sprigs.

Honey- and Soy-marinated Wood Pigeon Breasts with Spiced Quinoa

My restaurant, The Kitchin, is closed every Monday, so I'll be cooking at home and I often make this dish for the family. It's really important to me that I get the kids enjoying and eating as many different foods as possible. By bringing the honey and soy marinade into the dish, the kids love it, and it is a firm favourite in our house. You can, of course, use chicken instead, but do try pigeon, especially if you or someone you're cooking for hasn't tried it before.

─── SERVES 4 ───

4 tablespoons clear honey

2 tablespoons soy sauce

2 limes, halved

4 wood pigeon breasts, skinned and cut into thick strips

olive oil

1 fresh red chilli, deseeded and sliced

1½ teaspoons sesame seeds

small handful coriander sprigs, finely chopped

sea salt and freshly cracked black pepper

For the quinoa and pumpkin

olive oil

200g pumpkin, peeled, deseeded and chopped

1 garlic clove, chopped

½ onion, finely chopped

1 teaspoon finely peeled and chopped fresh ginger

200g quinoa, well rinsed and drained

freshly squeezed juice of 1 lime

500ml Chicken Stock (page 279) or vegetable stock, boiling

50g sultanas

1 spring onion, trimmed and sliced

Marinate the pigeon breast for 2–6 hours before cooking. Mix the honey and soy sauce together in a non-reactive bowl. Squeeze in the lime juice, then drop in the lime shells, add the pigeon strips and stir to coat in the marinade. Cover and chill until required.

Meanwhile, prepare the quinoa and pumpkin. Heat a large well-seasoned sauté or frying pan over a medium-high heat, then add a thin layer of olive oil. When it is hot, add the pumpkin and sauté for 2–3 minutes until it starts to soften. Add the garlic, onion and ginger with a pinch of salt, and continue sautéing until the onion is softened, but not coloured.

Add the quinoa and lime juice and continue stirring for a further minute. Add the boiling stock and leave the quinoa to simmer, uncovered, for 20–25 minutes, stirring occasionally, until it is tender. Season with salt and pepper, then stir in the sultanas and spring onion. Transfer to a bowl and leave to cool slightly to serve warm.

When you're ready to cook the pigeon breasts, wipe out the pan and heat it over a medium-high heat, then add a splash of oil. When it's hot, season the breasts with salt and pepper, the add them to the pan and sauté for 2–3 minutes. Add the marinade and continue stirring until the pigeon is cooked the way you like.

Remove the pigeon pieces and keep hot. Boil the marinade until it reduces by half, then stir in the red chilli and sesame seeds and simmer for 1 minute. Return the pigeon pieces to the pan, add the coriander and gently stir everything together. Adjust the seasoning with salt and pepper, if necessary, then serve with the quinoa and pumpkin.

Wood Pigeons and Plums Cooked in Red Wine with Soft Polenta

This is a really deep, rich and flavoursome dish. It's perfect on a dark winter's night with a fire burning. In a way, this recipe is a bit like cooking a coq au vin, but with the more gamy pigeon it works a treat. I love to serve this with polenta, as the soft grains soak up the wonderful sauce.

SERVES 2

50g plain flour

2 oven-ready wood pigeons, halved with the breasts and legs attached – ask your butcher to do this

olive oil

100g smoked lardons

6 black peppercorns

2 carrots, peeled and diced

2 celery sticks, diced

2 garlic cloves, chopped

1 bouquet garni

1 onion, chopped

500ml full-bodied red wine

400ml Game Stock (page 279)

200g plums, quartered and stoned

chopped flat-leaf parsley, to garnish

sea salt and freshly cracked black pepper

For the soft polenta

420ml milk, plus extra as needed

50g butter

freshly grated nutmeg

100g fine polenta

25g Parmesan cheese, freshly grated (optional)

The polenta can be made a couple of hours in advance for reheating just before serving, but it will probably become firm so you'll have to soften it again with extra milk. Bring the milk to the boil in a heavy-based saucepan, then add half the butter and nutmeg to taste. Now whisk in the polenta, and be aware it will thicken very quickly. Keep whisking the polenta over a low heat for 35–40 minutes until you can't taste any grains. If it is too thick, stir in a little extra milk.

Whisk in the remaining butter and cheese, if using. Season with salt, if necessary, but if you've added the cheese it might not be necessary. Set aside.

When you are ready to cook the pigeons, preheat the oven to 180°C Fan/200°C/ Gas Mark 6. Put the flour in a tray and season with salt and pepper. Pat the pigeon portions dry, then dust them with flour, shaking off the excess.

Heat a flameproof casserole over a medium-high heat, then add a good splash of oil. When it is hot, add the pigeon portions, skin side down, and fry until well coloured. Remove them from the casserole and set aside.

Add a little more oil to the casserole, then add the lardons and sauté until they have rendered their fat and are caramelised. Add the peppercorns, carrots, celery, garlic, bouquet garni and onion, and continue sautéing for a further 2–3 minutes until the vegetables are beginning to colour and soften.

Add the red wine to the casserole, stirring to deglaze the casserole, and boil until it reduces by half. Season the pigeon portions with salt and pepper and add them to the casserole with the game stock. The birds should be submerged, so add a little extra stock, if necessary. Cover the casserole and bring the liquid to the boil, then transfer the casserole to the oven for 1½–2 hours until the meat is tender enough to flake from the bones.

Remove the pigeon portions from the casserole and keep hot.

Strain the cooking juices into a saucepan, pressing down to extract as much flavour as possible, then boil until the juices are reduced by at least half and to a consistency you like. Stir in the plums and continue boiling until they are tender, then adjust the seasoning with salt and pepper, if necessary.

Reheat the polenta while the plums are cooking, adding extra milk, if necessary, to return it to a soft consistency, adjust the seasoning.

Serve the pigeon portions with the red wine sauce and plums spooned over, sprinkled with parsley, and the soft polenta alongside.

Pigeon, Lentil and Spelt Cheeseburgers

Pigeon and pulses are a natural marriage, but by combining both in a burger, I've created a really fun dish that everyone of all ages will enjoy. If you are ever looking for a good vegetarian dish just remove the pigeon and change the chicken stock to vegetable stock and you'll have a great veggie burger.

— SERVES 4 —

100g Puy lentils
100g spelt
400ml Chicken Stock (page 279)
100g carrots, peeled and grated
100g porridge oats
4 wood pigeon breasts, skinned and finely chopped
4 teaspoons finely chopped parsley
4 teaspoons finely chopped rosemary needles
olive oil for brushing the grill or pan
4 slices of cheddar cheese – my favourite comes from the Isle of Mull
sea salt and freshly cracked black pepper

To serve
4 burger buns, split
8 oakleaf salad leaves
1 plum tomato, sliced
50g gherkins, drained and sliced

You can prepare the burger mixture and shape the burgers up to a day in advance, then wrap them in clingfilm and chill until about 15 minutes before you cook.

Rinse the lentils and spelt under cold running water, then transfer them to a heavy-based saucepan with the chicken stock. Bring to the boil, then reduce the heat slightly and leave to gently boil, covered, for 30–40 minutes until both are tender. Season with salt.

Remove the pan from the heat, but do not drain. Set the lentils and spelt aside to cool slightly in the stock, then add the carrots, oats, pigeon breasts, parsley and rosemary, and mix together. The mixture should start to bind together, but if it is too crumbly add more oats. Fry a small amount in a well-seasoned pan to taste, then season with salt and pepper.

When the mixture is cool, lightly wet your hands and shape it into 4 equal-sized burgers, each about 2.5cm thick.

You can either barbecue or pan-fry the burgers. If you want to barbecue them, first light a barbecue and leave the coals until they are glowing and grey. Lightly grease the rack. Barbecue the burgers for 3–4 minutes, then carefully turn them over and move them to a slightly cooler part of the grill and cook for a further 3–4 minutes until done to your liking. Add the burger buns, cut side down to the rack and lightly toast.

Alternatively, preheat the grill to high and heat a large well-seasoned sauté or frying pan over a high heat, then add a thin layer of oil. When the oil is hot, add the burgers and cook for 3–4 minutes on each side until done to your liking. Put the burger buns, cut side up, under the grill and lightly toast.

Top each burger with a slice of cheese and either continue barbecuing or place under the hot grill until the cheese melts.

Divide the lettuce leaves and burgers among the buns, then top with the tomatoes, more lettuce leaves and gherkins.

Roasted Woodcock on Toast

Woodcock is the most beautiful bird but it needs to be treated with respect. Incredibly, any shot woodcock will always have a clean gut as they empty their bowels as they fly, so this is why, in this recipe, we cook the bird whole with its intestines intact.

SERVES 4

4 bacon rashers, each cut in half
2 woodcocks, 250g each, plucked and
    left whole with heads on
olive oil
1 teaspoon finely chopped shallot
10g foie gras (optional)
splash of brandy
4 thin bread slices
1 quantity Wilted Spinach (page 276),
    hot, to serve
sea salt and freshly cracked black pepper

Preheat the oven to 200°C Fan/220°C/Gas Mark 7.

Lay 2 pieces of bacon along the back of each of the birds, from head to tail end. Press the legs and wings of the woodcock together, then draw the head around and run the beak through where the legs and wings cross. Season the birds all over with salt and pepper.

Heat a large well-seasoned, ovenproof sauté or frying pan over a medium-high heat, then add a splash of oil. When it is hot, add the birds and colour on all sides. Turn the birds breast-side up, then transfer the pan to the oven and roast the birds for 6–8 minutes, basting several times, until the juices run clear when you use a small needle to pierce the thickest part of a leg.

Remove the birds from the pan and set aside to rest covered with kitchen foil. Do not turn off the oven or discard the cooking juices in the pan.

After the birds have rested, remove the stomach, intestines, heart and liver from each, discarding the stomach and intestines. Finely chop the livers and hearts and place in a bowl. Add the shallot and foie gras, if using, and mix together. Stir in a splash of the brandy and season with salt and pepper.

Remove the head from each woodcock, then split each head lengthways through the middle to expose the brain, a delicacy. Remove the breasts and legs from the birds and set aside, keep hot.

Meanwhile, toast the bread on both sides. Spread the heart and liver mixture over the hot toast, then place the toast in the oven for 3 minutes.

To serve, place the breasts and legs on top of the pieces of toast and add a split head to each plate. Garnish with the wilted spinach and serve.

Woodcock Breakfast, or My Take on Scotch Woodcock

I was lucky enough to have this dish for breakfast once at a shoot and it's a food memory that will stay with me forever. I love the way the salty, thinly cut anchovies work with the woodcock and scrambled eggs. If you have the opportunity to try this, give it a go.

SERVES 4

2 bacon rashers, each cut in half

2 woodcocks, 250g each, plucked and left whole with the heads on

vegetable oil

4 sourdough bread slices

butter for spreading

4 canned anchovy fillets, drained and chopped

sea salt and freshly cracked black pepper

For the scrambled eggs

6 eggs

30ml milk

10g butter

1 teaspoon chopped marjoram

Preheat the oven to 200°C Fan/220°C/Gas Mark 7.

Lay a piece of bacon along the back of each of the birds, from head to tail end. Use kitchen string to tie the legs together and secure the bacon in place, keeping the head on. Season the birds with salt and pepper to taste.

Heat a large well-seasoned, ovenproof sauté or frying pan over a medium-high heat, then add the oil. When it is hot, add the birds and colour them on all sides. Turn the birds breast-side up, then transfer the pan to the oven and roast the birds for 6–8 minutes, basting several times, until the juices run clear when you use a small needle to pierce the thickest part of a leg.

Remove the birds from the oven and set aside to rest for 5 minutes covered with foil. Remove the stomach, intestines, heart and liver from each. Depending on how adventurous you are, you can save the hearts and livers to serve. And, if you're feeling really adventurous, remove the head from each woodcock, then split each head lengthways through the middle to expose the brain, a delicacy. Remove the breasts with the bacon from each bird, then cut each breast in half and keep hot. Keep the bacon hot, too.

Meanwhile, toast the bread and keep hot while you make the scrambled eggs.

Whisk the eggs and milk together in a large bowl, then season with salt and pepper. Heat a large well-seasoned sauté or frying pan over a medium heat. Add the butter and when it melts, add the eggs and whisk constantly until they are lightly set. Remove the pan from the heat and keep whisking – I do not like them over-cooked. Stir in the marjoram.

To serve, butter the hot toast and top with the scrambled eggs. Top each with chopped anchovy pieces, then add the breast pieces and serve with the bacon – and the heads, hearts and livers, if you want.

Woodcock on Hay

Cooking meat on hay is nothing new. Chefs have been doing it for generations, using lamb, chicken and other meats, and it works fantastically well with woodcock, too. The best place to get hold of hay is from your local pet shop, but make sure you get the clean eating hay and not the bedding hay. I just love the smell of this dish as you take the lid off the pot.

— SERVES 4 —

4 pancetta slices, each folded in half

4 oven-ready woodcock, each about 250g

olive oil

½ bunch of fresh thyme

200g clean hay

1 oak leaf lettuce head, quartered, to serve

50g walnuts, chopped, to serve

50ml walnut oil, to serve

sea salt and freshly cracked black pepper

For the dressing

1 tablespoon sherry vinegar

1 teaspoon Dijon mustard

1 teaspoon chopped parsley

1 teaspoon finely chopped shallot

Preheat the oven to 200°C Fan/220°C/Gas Mark 7.

Lay a piece of folded pancetta along the back of each of the birds, from head to tail end. Use kitchen string to tie the legs together and secure the pancetta in place, keeping the head on. Season the birds with salt and pepper.

Heat a large flameproof casserole over a medium-high heat, then add a good splash of oil. When it is hot, add the birds and colour them on all sides. Remove the birds and set aside.

Add a little more oil to the casserole. Add the thyme sprigs and let them flavour the oil, then add the hay and spread it in a thick layer. Leave the pan on the hob over a low heat for the heat to penetrate the hay, then add the birds, breast side up, and cover the pan.

Transfer the pan to the oven and roast the birds for 6–8 minutes, basting several times, until the juices run clear when you use a small needle to pierce the thickest part of a leg. Remove the birds from the oven and leave to rest for 5 minutes covered with kitchen foil.

Meanwhile, to make the dressing, place the vinegar, mustard, parsley and shallots in a large non-reactive bowl and mix together. Add the lettuce leaves and toss with the dressing.

After the woodcock have rested, remove the breasts for each bird. Divide the oak leaf lettuce among 4 plates. Add the breasts, sprinkle the salad with walnuts and drizzle with the walnut oil.

Snipe Skewers

In the recipe, I've used the snipe beaks as skewers, but, of course, you can use a standard wood skewer, and you can also change the meat to another game bird if you don't have snipe. This is a really fun dish to serve with pre-dinner drinks for something a little bit different.

SERVES 4

4 oven-ready snipe, 170g each
8 pancetta slices
8 prunes, stoned
4 strong rosemary sprigs
olive oil
sea salt and freshly cracked black pepper

Once these skewers are assembled, they can be covered with clingfilm and chilled for up to a day. Remove them from the fridge 15 minutes before cooking so they return to room temperature.

Using a boning knife, and working with one snipe at a time, remove the breasts from the bird and set aside. Cut off the heads and set aside so the beaks can be used as the skewers. Repeat with the remaining snipe. (The carcasses can be used to make a game stock (page 279). And, if you aren't inclined to make a stock now, they can be frozen until required.)

Gently remove the skin from each breast, then season the pieces lightly with salt and pepper. Lay a pancetta slice on the work surface and top with a breast, a prune and a few rosemary needles, then roll up, as if making pigs in a blanket. Repeat to use the remaining breasts pieces and prunes, adding rosemary to each.

Spear 2 of the pancetta rolls with a beak. Continue to make 4 skewers in total.

Heat 2 large well-seasoned sauté or frying pans over a medium-high heat. Brush the surface with oil, add the skewers and cook for 2 minutes on each side, turning once, until the pancetta is crisp and the juices run clear when you use a small needle to pierce the thickest part of a leg, and then serve.

Woodcock and Pumpkin Soup

I love this dish, as it brings a lot of wow to the table when I serve it in a hollowed-out pumpkin, but, of course, there is still as much wow-factor in the flavour when it's served in a bowl. What I particularly love about this dish is that every spoon has a different flavour and texture as you work your way through the woodcock, croûtons, crispy ham and the lovely velvety soup.

SERVES 4

1kg pumpkin piece, plus a large whole
    pumpkin to serve from (optional)
olive oil
1 onion, sliced
1 teaspoon ground cinnamon
1 star anise
1 teaspoon clear honey
1 litre Chicken Stock (page 279)
4 woodcock breasts
4 Parma ham slices
sage leaves, to garnish
sea salt and freshly cracked black pepper

For the sourdough croûtons
150g sourdough, cut into thumb-size
    pieces
olive oil

I like to serve this with chunky sourdough croûtons, which will keep in an airtight container for up to 3 days. To make the croûtons, preheat the oven to 200°C Fan/220°C/Gas Mark 7. Place the bread chunks on a baking sheet and toss with a generous splash of olive oil so they are well coated. Place the baking sheet in the oven and bake for 8–10 minutes until the croûtons are golden brown and crispy. Tip on to a plate lined with kitchen paper, lightly season with salt and leave to cool before storing.

The soup can be made up to a day in advance. To make the soup, remove the skin and seeds from the 1kg piece of pumpkin, then dice the flesh.

Heat a heavy-based saucepan over a medium-high heat, then add about 2 tablespoons of oil. Add the pumpkin and stir for 2–3 minutes until it is beginning to soften. Add the onion, cinnamon and star anise, and season with salt and pepper. Continue stirring until the onion is softened, then add in the honey and stir for a further minute.

Pour in the chicken stock and bring to the boil. Lower the heat and simmer, partially covered, for 25–30 minutes until the pumpkin is tender. Transfer the contents of the pan to a blender or food processor and blitz until smooth. Return to the rinsed pan for reheating later.

Meanwhile, prepare the pumpkin shell if you are going to use it for serving from. Use the tip of a small knife to 'stencil' your way around the top of the pumpkin where you would like the lid to lift off, then insert the knife along that line and lift off the lid. Use a metal spoon to remove the pumpkin fibres and seeds. Set aside.

Just before you're ready to serve, season the woodcock breasts with salt and pepper. Heat a well-seasoned sauté or frying pan over a medium-high heat, then add a thin layer of oil. When it is hot, add the breasts, skin side down, and fry for 2 minutes. Turn them over and fry for a further 2 minutes, then set aside to rest for 5 minutes covered with kitchen foil.

Add the Parma ham slices to the oil remaining in the pan and fry, turning once, until crisp. Drain well on kitchen paper and set aside.

Add the sage leaves to the fat remaining in the pan and quickly fry until they are crispy. Drain on kitchen paper and season lightly with salt.

Reheat the soup and transfer it to the hollowed-out pumpkin, if using. Cut each woodcock breast in half and add to the soup, along with the croûtons, broken pieces of Parma ham and crispy sage leaves.

Woodcock, Snipe and Game Hot Pot

You can often buy game pie mix from butchers, game dealers or farmers' markets, basically a lovely mix of all types of game that has been prepared and is ready to use, which is what you want for this comforting dish. There is a bit of planning needed in this dish, as it's best to marinade the meat for 24 hours before cooking, but it's certainly worth the effort as the result is so delicious. I love to get the potatoes on top nice and crispy.

--- SERVES 4 ---

500g boneless venison, such as leg or shoulder, cut into bite-sized pieces

200g skinless pheasant or partridge breast meat, diced

100g woodcock breasts, skinned and finely chopped

100g snipe breasts, skinned and finely chopped

150g plain flour

olive oil

100g smoked lardons

200g celeriac, peeled and chopped

2 carrots, peeled and chopped

2 onions, chopped

2 garlic cloves, plus 1 extra, halved, for rubbing on the dish

1 tablespoon mixed chopped fresh rosemary and thyme

375ml dry red wine

400ml Game Stock (page 279)

6 black peppercorns, lightly crushed

25g butter, softened

750g waxy potatoes

25g Clarified Butter (page 276), melted

sea salt and freshly cracked black pepper

For the marinade

450ml full-bodied red wine

3 juniper berries, lightly crushed

1 bouquet garni

1 carrot, peeled and chopped

1 garlic clove, sliced

1 onion, chopped

Day 1

Place all the diced game in a large non-reactive bowl. Pour in the red wine for the marinade, then add the remaining marinade ingredients and mix together. Cover with clingfilm and chill for up to 24 hours.

Day 2

The next day, drain the game meat and discard the marinade ingredients. Pat the meat dry with a kitchen cloth. Season the flour with salt and pepper, then dust all the meat in the flour, shaking off the excess.

Heat a large flameproof casserole over a medium-high heat, then add a generous splash of oil. When it is hot, add the meat and colour on all sides. Drain well on kitchen paper and set aside. You will probably have to colour the meat in batches, so add extra oil as necessary.

Pour off the oil in the casserole. Return the casserole to the heat and a splash of fresh oil. When it is hot, add the lardons and sauté until they render their fat and are coloured all over. Add the celeriac, carrots, onions, garlic and rosemary and thyme with a pinch of salt, and sauté for a further 3–4 minutes until softened.

Return the game to the casserole. Add the red wine, stirring to deglaze, and boil until it reduces by half. Stir in the game stock and peppercorns. Return the liquid to the boil, then reduce the heat to low, cover the casserole and leave the game to simmer for 1½ hours.

Meanwhile, when the game has almost finished simmering, preheat the oven to 170°C Fan/190°C/Gas Mark 5 and lightly butter the inside of a 2-litre ovenproof serving dish. Rub the cut garlic around. Peel the potatoes and thinly slice them. A mandolin is ideal for this if you have one.

Put the game mixture in the dish, then top with the potato slices. Brush the slices with clarified butter, then cover with kitchen foil, shiny side down. Place the dish on a baking sheet, transfer to the oven and bake for 1½ hours.

Increase the oven temperature to 200°C Fan/220°C/Gas Mark 7 and take the foil off the top, brushing with clarified butter again. Continue baking for 15 minutes, or until the potatoes are golden brown. Set aside to rest, covered with kitchen foil, for 10 minutes before serving.

Woodcock à la Ficelle

Let's be honest, this is a dish for the more adventurous cook, but boy is it fun to do. It's all about the preparation and getting the fire to the right temperature. I use metal wire from the DIY shop to tie the birds, which then allows me to move them up and down easily during the cooking process. I find there is something really magical about cooking on a fire outdoors and the family love it.

— SERVES 4 —

4 woodcock, 250g each, plucked and left whole with head on
4 sourdough bread slices
sea salt and freshly cracked black pepper

First set up your barbecue with metal poles that you can suspend the birds from, as I've done in the photograph. Make sure the poles are spaced wide enough apart so the birds have enough space to hang and rotate as they cook. Next light a barbecue and leave the coals until they are glowing, with a 'soft' heat. As the fat drips onto the coals they will flare up, but start with a soft heat.

To prepare the birds, cover the feet and beak of each bird with kitchen foil to prevent them from burning. Attach a thick string or a steel cord to the beak and head of each woodcock that will be used to hang the birds about 10–20 inches above the coals – the idea is that the birds will rotate in the heat as they cook. If using a steel cord it should be flexible so you can higher and lower the bird. Set aside until the coals are ready: the coals should be glowing, and there should be no flames.

When the coals are glowing, attach the birds to the poles and cook for 10–12 minutes, raising them higher if they are cooking too fast.

Now place the bread in 3 blini pans (or a heavy-based pan) underneath the birds so the wonderful juices drop on to the bread. The birds will take roughly another 10–15 minutes cooking, which depends on the heat of the fire, until the juices run clear when you use a small needle to pierce the thickest part of a leg.

When the birds are cooked, lightly toast the bread in the pan sitting on the coals. Serve the breast meat and legs on the toast.

Snipe Jacket Potatoes à la Koffmann

I once saw the great Pierre Koffman cook this for some of his friends at his restaurant, La Tante Claire. It's a very clever and effective piece of cooking. I love how all the lovely snipe cooking juices melt into the soft potato, making it an incredible eating experience that you won't forget cooking … and your friends won't forget eating.

—— SERVES 4 ——

250g rock salt

4 large baking potatoes, such as Maris Piper, well scrubbed

8 black peppercorns

olive oil

4 snipe, 170g each, plucked but left whole with the head on

50g butter

4 garlic cloves, peeled and cracked

4 thyme sprigs

1 tablespoon chopped flat-leaf parsley

sea salt

Preheat the oven to 200°C Fan/220°C/Gas Mark 7. Spread the rock salt in a layer in a roasting tray large enough to hold the potatoes.

Prick the potatoes all over with the tip of a sharp knife, then rest them in the rock salt. Place the tray in the oven and bake the potatoes for 1½–2 hours, depending on their size, until they are very tender and a knife slides in without any resistance. Remove them from the tray and set aside. Do not turn off the oven.

Meanwhile, use a pestle and mortar to coarsely crack the peppercorns, then season the snipe all over with salt and the cracked pepper.

Heat a large heavy-based, ovenproof frying pan over a medium-high heat, then add a splash of oil. When it is hot, add the snipe to the pan and fry to colour all over. Add the butter, garlic and thyme, and when the butter foams, baste the snipe well. Remove the pan from the heat.

Make an incision in each of the potatoes and squeeze to open them out. Spoon a little of the butter from the pan into each potato. Top each with a snipe, then add a garlic clove and thyme sprig from the pan.

Return the potatoes to the tray with the rock salt and spoon the remaining butter over them. Place the tray in the oven and roast the birds for a further 8–10 minutes until the juices run clear when you use a small needle to pierce the thickest part of a leg.

Remove the snipe-topped potatoes from the oven and set aside to rest for 5 minutes covered with kitchen foil. Sprinkle with parsley just before serving.

Mallard Breasts Baked in a Salt Crust

Roasting an ingredient in a salt crust is a very traditional way of cooking and is probably better known as a way of cooking fish to keep it tender. Using mallard breasts, however, also works fantastically well. It's important, however, not to skin the breasts, and to place the breasts on top of each other flesh to flesh, so only the skin is exposed to the salt, which helps to protect the meat. For a bit of theatre, crack the salt crust in front of your guests.

— SERVES 4 —

2 tablespoons olive oil

4 large, plump mallard breasts, 75 –100g each

For the salt pastry

1 teaspoon black peppercorns

1kg fine sea salt

1kg coarse sea salt

1 tablespoon chopped rosemary needles

1 teaspoon thyme leaves

2 free-range egg whites, beaten

100ml water

Preheat the oven to 220°C Fan/240°C/Gas Mark 9. Cut out two pieces of 30 x 15cm greaseproof paper and set aside on 2 baking sheets.

Heat a large well-seasoned sauté or frying pan over a medium heat, then add the oil. When it is hot, add the duck breasts and fry on the skin side for 1 minute, then turn over and fry for a further 30 seconds. Remove from the pan and leave to cool completely on kitchen paper while you make the salt pastry.

To make the pastry, use a pestle and mortar to coarsely crack all the peppercorns. Place the cracked pepper into a sieve and shake off any excess powder, keeping the remaining cracked pepper. Place the fine and coarse salt in to a bowl and mix together with the cracked peppercorns, rosemary and thyme. Make a well in the centre, add the egg whites with the water and mix together until everything is combined.

Divide the pastry into 4 portions and spread out 1 portion on each piece of paper, patting out each until it is slightly larger than the size of a breast. Place 2 breasts on top of each layer of salt pastry, flesh sides together, then add the remaining salt pastry, mounding it tightly over the breasts. It's important that the edges are sealed and there aren't any air gaps.

Place the baking sheets in the oven and bake the duck breasts for 12–14 minutes, depending on their size, until the salt crust is firm and light brown. Remove from the oven and set aside to rest for 8 minutes.

To serve, carefully crack the salt and remove the breasts, wiping off any excess salt.

Peppered Wild Mallard Breasts with Girolles, Shallots and Spinach

Mallard is only in season from early September until the end of January, which is a relevantly short time, which makes eating the wild duck even more special. I love to coat the breasts in crushed peppercorns and quickly pan-fry them so the flesh is still pink. I then serve them with sautéed wild mushrooms and a delicious shallot marmalade, which works with most meats and adds a special touch.

A variation on this recipe is to use eight teal breasts, instead of the duck breasts. Pan-fry them for 2 minutes on the skin side, then turn them over and pan-fry for a further minute.

———————————————— SERVES 4 ————————————————

2 tablespoons black peppercorns

4 mallard breasts, 75–100g each

50g duck fat

olive oil

100g shallots, sliced

1 tablespoon sherry vinegar

1 teaspoon finely chopped garlic and parsley

Wilted Spinach (page 276), hot, to serve

sea salt and freshly cracked black pepper

For the sautéed girolles

olive oil

100g girolles, trimmed and wiped

Using a pestle and mortar, crush the black peppercorns gently. Place the crushed pepper in to a sieve and shake off any excess powder, keeping just the crushed peppercorns, then set aside.

Using a small sharp knife, remove the skin from the mallard breasts, then season the breasts with salt and coat in the cracked black pepper, pressing it on firmly. Set aside.

To cook the girolles, heat a well-seasoned sauté pan over a medium-high heat, then add a little oil. Add the girolles with a pinch of salt and sauté until they are tender and absorb the liquid they give off. Set aside and keep hot.

Cook the wilted spinach, following the instructions on page 276 and keep hot.

To cook the breasts, wipe out the pan the girolles were cooked in and heat over a medium-high heat, then add the duck fat. When it melts, add the breasts, skin-side down, and fry for 3–4 minutes, turning once half-way through, until they are nicely coloured. Remove the breasts from the pan and set aside to rest for 5 minutes covered with kitchen foil.

Wipe out the pan. Return it to the heat and add a splash of oil. When it is hot, add the shallots and sauté for 1–2 minutes until softened. Add the sherry vinegar, stirring to deglaze the pan, and leave until it evaporates. Stir in the garlic and parsley and adjust the seasoning with salt and pepper.

Serve the breasts with the girolles, shallots and wilted spinach alongside.

Asian-flavoured Wild Duck Broth and Noodles

Never throw away the carcass of anything! With a little inspiration, you can easily make a meal out of not very much, as this recipe perfectly illustrates. By adding some good chicken or duck stock, spices, aromatics and soy sauce and cooking everything in one pot, you will be amazed to discover just how much depth of flavour can be achieved. If you don't have a duck carcass to make the broth with, you'll still have an excellent result using all chicken stock.

SERVES 4

2 cooked mallard duck carcases, about 500g in total

vegetable oil

6 green cardamom pods, lightly crushed

2 celery sticks, chopped

1 carrot, peeled and chopped

1 onion, sliced

1 star anise

1 litre Chicken Stock (page 279) or duck stock

1 teaspoon peeled and chopped root ginger

2 fresh red chillies, deseeded and chopped

2 tablespoons chopped coriander stalks

1 tablespoon soy sauce, or to taste

freshly cracked black pepper

To serve

300g egg noodles

280g cooked duck meat, shredded

2 spring onions, finely sliced

1 fresh red chilli, deseeded and sliced

15g root ginger, peeled and cut into very thin strips

fresh coriander leaves

The duck broth can be made up to 2 days in advance and chilled until required. Carefully remove the cooked meat from the carcasses and set aside. Using a large knife or kitchen scissors, cut the carcass in to small pieces.

Heat a large heavy-based saucepan over a medium-high heat, then add the oil. When the oil is hot, add the chopped carcasses and sauté for 4–5 minutes until they are browned. Add the cardamom pods, celery, carrot, onion and star anise, and sauté for a further 3–4 minutes, shaking the pan occasionally to prevent sticking, until the vegetables are softened.

Pour in the chicken stock. Add the ginger, red chillies and coriander stalks, cover the pan and bring the stock to the boil. Reduce the heat to medium-low, partially cover the pan and leave the stock to simmer for 35–40 minutes, skimming the surface as necessary, until the bones are tender and break easily. If you think the stock is a bit weak tasting, uncover, return it to the boil and boil until it reduces by one-third.

Strain the stock through a chinois or fine sieve and discard the flavouring ingredients. Return the stock to the washed pan and season with pepper. At this point it can be left to cool completely and chilled until required.

Just before you're ready to serve, bring the stock to the boil and adjust the seasoning with soy sauce. Add the egg noodles and boil according to the packet instructions until tender. Add the cooked duck meat to heat through at the last minute.

Divide the noodles and duck meat among 4 bowls. Ladle over the hot broth, then sprinkle each bowl with spring onions, chilli, ginger and coriander leaves.

Cauliflower Soup with Sautéed Duck Hearts and Parma Ham

Cauliflower soup is smooth and comforting when made properly, and for me that means it is rich and creamy with that wonderful flavour of cauliflower coming through. It's a versatile dish which goes with just about anything, as I'm highlighting in this sophisticated recipe. Anyone who knows me knows I don't like to waste anything, so leftover mallard hearts from other recipes are sautéed and served in this hearty soup. (And, if you don't have any hearts, you should be able to get them from your butcher.) My idea of food heaven.

SERVES 4

50g Clarified Butter (page 276)
olive oil
1 onion, thinly sliced
800g cauliflower florets, thinly sliced
1 litre Chicken Stock (page 279) or
   vegetable stock
150ml whipping cream
sea salt and freshly cracked black pepper

To serve
100g duck hearts
100g cauliflower florets or Romanesco
   cauliflower
olive oil
8 Parma ham slices
1 teaspoon chopped garlic
1 teaspoon chopped parsley

Heat a large heavy-based saucepan over a medium-high heat, then melt the clarified butter with a splash of oil. When the butter is foaming, add the onion, reduce the heat to low, cover the pan and leave the onion to sweat for 3–4 minutes, shaking the pan occasionally to prevent sticking, until it is softened, but not coloured.

Add the cauliflower to the pan with a pinch of salt. Re-cover the pan and leave the cauliflower to sweat for a further 3–4 minutes, shaking the pan occasionally, until it is just beginning to become tender. Add the stock and cream, and simmer, partially covered, for 15 minutes, or until the cauliflower is tender.

Transfer the mixture to a blender or food processor and blend until smooth and velvety. Return to the washed pan and season with salt and pepper.

Meanwhile, prepare the ingredients to serve with the soup. Using a small sharp knife, clean the hearts to remove any blood clots or sinew and cut each in half, then set aside.

Bring a saucepan of salted water to the boil. Add the 100g of cauliflower florets and blanch for 1–2 minutes until just tender. Drain well, then refresh under cold running water to stop the cooking. Pat dry with kitchen paper and set aside.

Heat a well-seasoned sauté or frying pan over medium-high heat, then add a splash of oil. When the oil is hot, add the Parma ham slices and fry, turning once, until crisp. Drain well on kitchen paper and set aside.

Add the hearts to the pan that you just fried the ham in over a medium heat. Season with salt and pepper and sauté for 2 minutes for tender rare to medium-rare meat. Add the blanched cauliflower florets to the pan to heat through for about 1 minute, gently stirring. Stir in the garlic and parsley.

Reheat the soup, and adjust the seasoning with salt and pepper, if necessary, but remember the Parma ham is salty. Serve the soup in bowls and garnish with broken pieces of crispy Parma ham, the hearts and cauliflower florets.

Mallard en Croûte

Mallard en croûte, as the French say, is wild duck in pastry to us Brits, and is one of my favourite dishes. We all seem to love any meat in pastry combination, and why not? I suppose this dish is a slight twist on a beef Wellington, but by adding cabbage it's the perfect mixture for mallard. If you scale up the quantities, this dish is ideal for dinner parties, as all the work is in the preparation, so you'll have time to spend with your guests.

SERVES 2

1 oven-ready mallard, about 600g

½ savoy cabbage, cored and very finely shredded

olive oil

50g thinly cut smoked lardons

½ onion, thickly sliced

½ garlic clove, crushed to a purée

100g crépinette (pork caul fat), rinsed

100g sliced pancetta

200g puff pastry, thawed if frozen

plain flour for rolling out the pastry

2 free-range egg yolks, beaten

sea salt and freshly cracked black pepper

Start by using a boning knife to remove the wishbone from the duck, then cut off the legs and remove the 2 breasts from the crown. Carefully remove the skin from the breasts and legs, then cut out the thigh bone and separate the thigh meat from the drumstick. Carefully remove the bone from the thighs, keeping the piece of meat whole. (You don't need the drumsticks for this recipe, so they can be used in another recipe, or frozen to make stock with, and the carcasses can be used to make stock with or frozen until you're in the mood or have time to make stock.)

Bring a large saucepan of salted water to the boil. Add the cabbage and blanch for 2–3 minutes until it just starts to wilt, then immediately drain. Refresh under cold running water to stop the cooking and set the colour. Pat dry with a kitchen cloth and set aside.

Meanwhile, heat a large well-seasoned sauté or frying pan over a medium-high heat, then add a splash of oil. When it is hot, add the lardons and sauté until they render their fat and are coloured all over. Add the onion and garlic and continue sautéing for a further minute, or until the onion starts to soften. Add the cabbage and continue sautéing for 4–5 minutes until it is tender. Remove the pan from the heat and set aside.

Cut the crépinette into 2 equal-sized portions, and lay one piece on the work surface. Arrange half the sliced pancetta on top so it is the length of a duck breast. Season a breast with salt and pepper and place it on top of the pancetta. Add 2 generous tablespoons of the cabbage, then place a thigh on top. Roll the pancetta and crépinette around the duck and cabbage to make a thick sausage shape. Repeat with the other piece of crépinette and the remaining duck breast, thigh and cabbage. Set both duck parcels aside.

Divide the puff pastry into 2 equal-sized portions. Roll out each portion on a lightly floured surface with a lightly floured rolling pin into a 20 x 15cm rectangle about 3mm thick. Now place one of the duck parcels on a piece of puff pastry, rolling the pastry around until the duck and cabbage are completely covered. Lightly squeeze all the joins so the pastry is well sealed. Repeat with the remaining ingredients to make another duck parcel, then chill both of them for 20 minutes.

Continued on page 266

Meanwhile, preheat the oven to 200°C Fan/220°C/Gas Mark 7.

Brush each parcel with the beaten eggs. Roll out any trimmings, if you like, to make leaves for arranging on the parcels, securing them in position with the beaten eggs.

Place the pastry parcels on a baking sheet and bake for 16–17 minutes until the pastry is golden brown. Remove from the oven and leave to rest for 8 minutes before slicing.

Wild Duck Cabbage Balls

For this recipe I've used only wild duck, which would always be my first choice, but the recipe also works with any game bird if you were struggling to find wild duck. What's really clever here is that the leftover cooking liquid is used as the sauce. The sweetness of the Madeira cooked with the cabbage and game is sensational, so I suggest to baste the cabbage balls regularly during the cooking process to help maximise the flavour.

SERVES 8

---

2 tablespoons vegetable oil

50g smoked lardons

100g celeriac, peeled and finely chopped

2 celery sticks, chopped

2 garlic cloves, finely chopped

1 carrot, peeled and diced

1 shallot, finely chopped

50ml brandy

50ml Madeira

50ml port

500ml Game Stock (page 279)

1 bouquet garni

sea salt and freshly cracked black pepper

For the cabbage balls

15g butter

1 tablespoon olive oil

½ onion, chopped

½ garlic clove, chopped

½ teaspoon herbes de Provence

100g wild or button mushrooms, trimmed, wiped and chopped

25ml brandy

100g diced boneless, skinless mallard, teal or wigeon

100g minced pork belly fat

50g duck hearts and livers, well trimmed and finely chopped

25g dried breadcrumbs

25ml double cream

1 free-range egg, beaten

½ large Savoy cabbage

250g crépinette (pork caul fat), rinsed

To start the cabbage balls, heat a large well-seasoned sauté or frying pan over a medium-high heat, then melt the butter with the oil. When the butter is foaming, add the onion, garlic and dried herbs, lower the heat, cover the pan and leave the onion to sweat for 2–3 minutes, shaking the pan occasionally, until it is softened, but not coloured.

Add the mushrooms, re-cover the pan and continue sweating them for a further 2–3 minutes until they are tender. Add the brandy to the pan, stirring to deglaze the pan, and boil until it evaporates. Remove the pan from the heat and set aside for all the ingredients to cool.

Combine the duck meat, pork belly fat, the duck hearts and livers and the cool onion mixture in a large bowl. Add the breadcrumbs, cream and egg, and season with salt and pepper, then mix well together. Fry a small amount in a well-seasoned pan to taste and adjust the salt and pepper, if necessary.

Meanwhile, bring a large saucepan of water to the boil, then season with salt. Place a large bowl of iced water in the sink.

While the water is coming to the boil, cut off the root end of the cabbage and separate 8 large leaves. Try not to use the very green leaves, because they will be bitter. Add the leaves to the boiling water and blanch for 1–2 minutes until tender, then immediately drain and put in the iced water to stop the cooking and refresh. Drain again and pat dry with a kitchen cloth.

Use a small sharp knife to cut out the large central vein in each leaf to make them easier to roll. Cut the crépinette into 8 pieces, each about 15 x 15cm.

Divide the duck mixture into 8 equal-sized portions and roll into balls. Working with one leaf at a time, place a ball of stuffing in the centre of the leaf. Carefully pull the sides of the cabbage around the stuffing to make a round neat parcel. Gently wrap the ball in a piece of crépinette, then set aside. Repeat to stuff the remaining leaves. At this point the cabbage balls can be covered with clingfilm and chilled for 2–3 hours, or frozen for up to 3 months. (Thaw before cooking.)

Continued on page 269

When you're ready to cook, preheat the oven to 180°C Fan/200°C/Gas Mark 7.

Heat the oil in a large flameproof casserole over a medium-high heat, then add a splash of oil. When it is hot, add the lardons and sauté until they have rendered their fat and are lightly coloured all over. Add the celeriac, celery, garlic, carrot and shallot, and sauté for a further 2–3 minutes until all the vegetables are beginning to colour and soften.

Add the brandy, Madeira and port, stirring to deglaze the pan, and boil until the liquid evaporates. Add the game stock and bouquet garni and bring to the boil. Season with salt and pepper.

Carefully add the cabbage balls to the casserole. Cover the casserole, transfer it to the oven and braise the cabbage balls for 40–45 minutes, basting every 15 minutes. They are cooked through when you insert a metal skewer through the centre and it feels hot when you then put it on your lips. Serve the cabbage balls with the cooking liquid and the flavouring vegetables spooned round them.

Mallard Breasts with Carrot Tatins

Duck and orange go together like a horse and carriage. It is one of the best-known combinations in the culinary world, and it's easy to understand why! Instead of making the classic orange sauce here, which is not so easy for the home cook, I've come up with the idea of a carrot tatin to serve with the mallard breasts and orange segments. You'll find the individual tatin tins at good kitchen shops and online.

SERVES 4
---

4 mallard breasts, 75–100g each
2 tablespoons olive oil
sea salt and freshly cracked black pepper

For the carrot tatins

4 baby carrots, peeled and trimmed with
    some of the green stalks left in place
20g butter, melted
60g caster sugar
150g puff pastry, thawed if frozen
plain flour for rolling out the pastry
1 free-range egg yolk, beaten

To garnish

Orange Confit (page 277)
1 orange, peeled and segmented (use
    the orange peel to make the confit if
    you haven't already made it)
4 raw baby carrots, trimmed but with
    some stalk left, halved lengthways
wild watercress or ordinary watercress
    leaves

The carrot tatins require at least 20 minutes chilling and can be assembled up to 4 hours in advance and baked just before you cook the duck breasts. First bring a saucepan of salted water to boil and place a bowl of iced water in the sink. Add the carrots to the boiling water and blanch for 3–4 minutes until just tender, then drain well and immediately put them in the iced water. Now cut the carrots into batons to fit 10cm tatin moulds. Use a mould as a cutter for the carrots to get the correct size.

Preheat the grill to high. Brush the inside of 4 moulds with the melted butter. Divide the caster equally among the buttered moulds, making sure all the inner surfaces are covered, then tap out the excess. Put the moulds under the grill to caramelise the sugar and butter. Neatly arrange the carrots in the moulds on top of the caramel, then set aside.

Roll out the puff pastry on a lightly floured work surface with a lightly floured rolling pin until it is 1cm thick. Cut out four 10cm circles. Place them on a baking sheet or flat plate that will fit in your fridge. Cover with clingfilm and chill for at least 20 minutes, or up to 3 hours.

Meanwhile, preheat the oven 200°C Fan/220°C/Gas Mark 7.

Place a puff pastry circle on top of each tatin, gently pressing down and tucking in the edge. Brush the pastry with the beaten egg yolk. Place the tatins on a baking sheet and bake for 20–25 minutes until the puff pastry is golden brown.

While the tatins are baking, cook the duck breasts. Using a small sharp knife, score the skin of each breast in a criss-cross pattern, being careful not to cut into the flesh. Season the breasts all over with salt and pepper.

Heat a large well-seasoned sauté or frying pan over a medium-high, then add the oil. When it is hot, add the breasts, skin-side down, and fry for 4–5 minutes until the skin is nicely coloured. Turn them over and cook for a further 1–2 minutes, then remove from the pan. Set aside to rest for 5 minutes covered with kitchen foil.

While the breasts are resting, remove the tatins from the oven and loosen the pastry edges. Invert the tatins on to 4 serving plates so the pastry becomes the base under the carrots.

To serve, cut each breast into 3 or 4 pieces and arrange on top of a tatin. Garnish with strained pieces of orange confit, orange segments, halved raw carrots and wild watercress sprigs.

Spiced Teal with a Plum, Chicory and Radicchio Salad

Mallard is the largest and most-common wild duck, followed by widgeon and then my favourite, teal. You will find teal and other varieties of duck from game dealers (online even), farmers' markets or butchers. Teal is unique in the sense that it has the flavour of wild duck with a delicate and wonderfully tender meat. This recipe just goes to show how versatile it is and can be enjoyed in so many different ways.

SERVES 4

4 oven-ready teal, about 450g each
sea salt and freshly cracked black pepper

For the spice rub
2 teaspoons coriander seeds
2 teaspoons cumin seeds
1 teaspoon cardamom seeds
1 teaspoon fennel seeds
1 teaspoon black peppercorns
1 teaspoon dried pink peppercorns
1 teaspoon ground Szechuan pepper
30g light brown sugar
2 tablespoons soy sauce
4 teaspoons clear honey

For the plum, chicory and radicchio salad
2 chicory heads, separated into leaves
1 radicchio head, separated into leaves
1 bunch watercress sprigs
2 plums

Plan ahead to allow for at least 5 hours chilling time before cooking. Using a sharp knife, remove the wishbones from each teal, then pierce each bird all over.

Bring a large saucepan of water to the boil. One by one, dip the teal in the water for 30 seconds. Leave them to drain and cool completely on a wire rack, then cover with clingfilm and place in the fridge for at least 2 hours, but no more than 4 hours.

Meanwhile, to make the spice rub, use a pestle and mortar to crush the coriander, cumin, cardamom and fennel seeds and the black and pink peppercorns until a coarse powder forms. Transfer the spice powder to a bowl, add the Szechuan pepper, brown sugar, soy sauce and honey, then season with salt and stir together.

Remove the duck from the fridge and rub the coarse spice rub all over them. Return the teal to the fridge and leave for at least 3 hours or up to 4 hours. Do not discard the remaining spice rub.

When you're ready to cook, preheat the oven to 170°C Fan/190°C/Gas Mark 5 and remove the teal from the fridge in enough time for them to return to room temperature. Line a roasting tray with kitchen foil, shiny side up.

Rub each teal again with the remaining spice mixture. Place in a roasting tray and roast for 15 minutes for medium rare. Set aside and leave to rest covered with kitchen foil for 5 minutes. Do not discard the cooking juice in the roasting tray.

Make the salad while the birds are roasting. Put the chicory and radicchio leaves and watercress sprigs in a non-reactive bowl, and season lightly with salt and pepper, then toss together. Quarter the plums, removing the stones and add them to the bowl. At the last minute, add the cooking juices from the roasting tray for the dressing and toss again.

Divide the teal among 4 plates and serve each with a portion of the salad alongside.

Basics

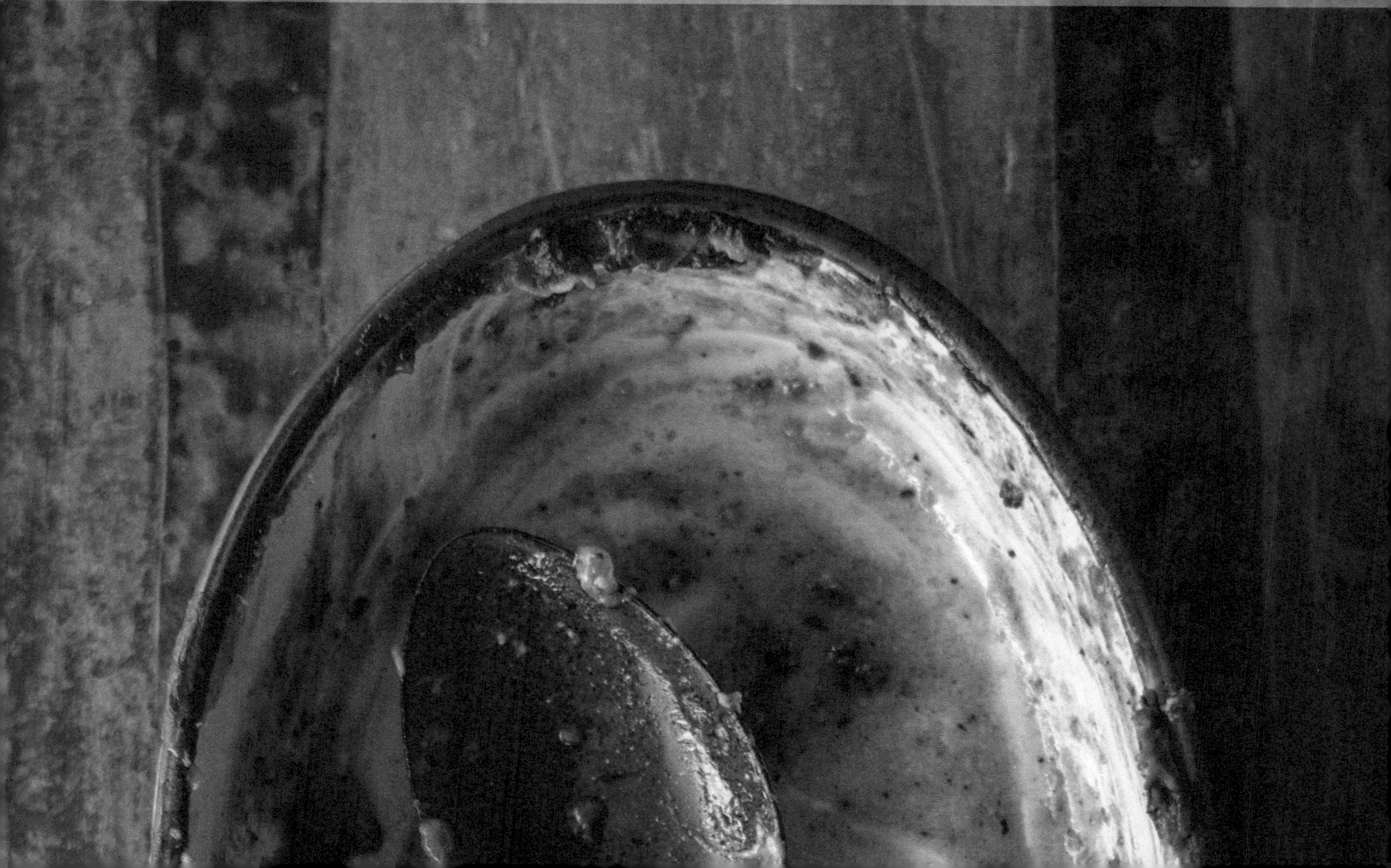

Wilted Spinach

300g spinach leaves
1 garlic clove, peeled but left whole
olive oil
sea salt

The wilted spinach takes less than 1 minute to cook. Rinse the spinach well, then shake dry. Spear the garlic clove with a fork. Heat a large well-seasoned frying pan over a medium-high heat, then add a splash of oil. When it is hot, add the spinach with just the water clinging to the leaves, season with a little salt and toss with the garlic fork until just wilted. This technique gives the spinach a mild garlic flavour, which I think is wonderful.

Clarified Butter

150g unsalted butter

Put the butter into a heavy-based saucepan and melt very gently over a low heat. The milk solids should separate out and fall to the bottom of the pan. Carefully put the clarified butter into a bowl, leaving the milk solids in the pan.

Mayonnaise

MAKES ABOUT 300ML

2 free-range medium egg yolks, at room
    temperature
1 teaspoon Dijon mustard
25ml white wine vinegar
250ml sunflower or vegetable oil
squeeze of lemon juice
sea salt

Put the egg yolks into a medium bowl with the Dijon mustard and white wine vinegar, and whisk together until evenly combined. Slowly drizzle in the oil, whisking continuously to emulsify the mixture. Once all the oil is added you should have a thick and glossy mayonnaise. Season with a squeeze of lemon and salt to taste.

Lemon Confit

2 lemons
100g caster sugar
300ml water

You can make the lemon confit up to 1 week in advance. Using a vegetable peeler, peel the lemon and squeeze 2 tablespoons of juice, then set it aside. Scrape any bitter white pith from the peel, then finely chop the peel.

Place the lemon peel pieces in a small saucepan with cold water to cover. Bring the water to the boil, then immediately drain and refresh the peel under cold water. Repeat this process 3 times.

Return the lemon pieces to the pan over a low heat. Add the sugar, water and lemon juice, stirring to dissolve the sugar, then bring to the boil, without stirring. Lower the heat and leave to simmer for 25–30 minutes until soft. Remove the pan from the heat and leave the peel pieces to cool in the syrup. The pieces will float in the syrup and you can leave them in a covered container at room temperature.

A variation: Orange Confit
Follow the recipe above, using the pared peel of 1 orange, 2 tablespoons of orange juice, 300ml water and 100g caster sugar. Store as above.

Beef Stock

2kg raw beef bones
2 tablespoons olive oil
1 carrot, peeled and roughly chopped
1 celery stalk, halved
1 onion, roughly chopped
½ garlic head, halved
3 tablespoons tomato purée
3.5 litres water
5 black peppercorns
2 thyme sprigs
1 bay leaf
sea salt

Preheat the oven to 200°C Fan/220°C/Gas Mark 7. Put the bones in a roasting tray, drizzle with 1 tablespoon of the oil and roast for 20 minutes, or until browned.

Meanwhile, heat a large well-seasoned stockpot or saucepan over a medium heat, then add the remaining 1 tablespoon of oil. When it is hot, add the carrot, celery, onion, and garlic, then turn the heat to very low. Cover the vegetables with a wet piece of greaseproof paper, cover the pan with a lid and leave them to sweat for 6–8 minutes until they are very tender. Add the tomato purée and stir for 1–2 minutes to cook out the raw flavour.

Add the roasted bones to the pan, then pour in the water and add the peppercorns, thyme sprigs, bay leaf and a pinch of salt. Bring to the boil, skimming the surface as necessary. Lower the heat and leave to simmer, partially covered, for 3–4 hours.

Remove and discard the bones, then strain the stock into a large bowl. Leave to cool completely, then cover and chill for up to 4 days. Remove the fat from the surface before using. The stock can also be frozen for up to 4 months.

Lamb Stock

2kg lamb bones
2 tablespoons olive oil
3 carrots, peeled and chopped
1 onion, chopped
1 fennel bulb, chopped
½ head of garlic, halved
½ red pepper
1 teaspoon ground cumin
1 teaspoon fennel seeds
3 tablespoons tomato purée
3.5 litres water
100ml dry white wine
1 bouquet garni

Preheat the oven to 200°C Fan/220°C/Gas Mark 7. Put the bones in a roasting tray, drizzle with 1 tablespoon of the oil and roast for 20 minutes, or until browned.

Meanwhile, heat a large well-seasoned stockpot or saucepan over a medium heat, then add the remaining 1 tablespoon of oil. When it is hot, add the carrots, onion, fennel and garlic, then turn the heat to very low. Cover the vegetables with a wet piece of greaseproof paper, cover the pan with a lid, turn the heat to very low and leave them to sweat for 6–8 minutes until they are very tender.

Add the red pepper, cumin and fennel seeds, and sweat for a further 1–2 minutes. Add the tomato purée and stir for 1–2 minutes to cook out the raw flavour.

Add the roasted bones to the pan, then pour in the water and white wine and add the bouquet garni. Bring to the boil, skimming the surface as necessary. Lower the heat and leave to simmer, partially covered, for 3–4 hours.

Remove and discard the bones, then strain the stock into a large bowl. Leave to cool completely, then cover and chill for up to 4 days. Remove the fat from the surface before using. The stock can also be frozen for up to 4 months.

Chicken Stock

MAKES ABOUT 2 LITRES

2kg raw chicken carcasses
1 tablespoon olive oil
3.5 litres water
2 carrots, peeled and roughly chopped
1 onion, roughly chopped
½ garlic head, halved
5 white peppercorns
2 thyme sprigs
1 bay leaf
sea salt

Preheat the oven to 200°C Fan/220°C/Gas Mark 7. Remove any excess fat from the chicken carcasses and roughly chop them up. Put the chicken carcass in a roasting tray and drizzle with the oil and roast for 20 minutes, or until browned.

Place the bones in a large saucepan and pour over the cold water. Bring to the boil, then lower the heat and simmer gently for 20 minutes, skimming frequently to remove impurities as they float to the surface.

Add the carrots, onion, garlic, peppercorns, thyme, bay leaf and a pinch of salt, then simmer, partially covered, for a further 1½ hours, topping up the water, if necessary.

Strain the stock through a chinois or fine sieve into a bowl, then leave to cool completely and chill until required. Remove any fat from the surface before using. Store the stock in a covered container in the fridge for up to 4 days, or freeze for up to 4 months.

Game Stock

MAKES ABOUT 2 LITRES

2kg raw game bones or carcass
2 tablespoons olive oil
1 carrot, peeled and roughly chopped
1 celery stalk, halved
1 onion, roughly chopped
½ garlic head, halved
3.5 litres water
5 black peppercorns
2 thyme sprigs
1 bay leaf
sea salt

Preheat the oven to 200°C Fan/220°C/Gas Mark 7. Put the bones in a roasting tray, drizzle with 1 tablespoon of the oil and roast for 20 minutes, or until browned.

Meanwhile, heat a large well-seasoned stockpot or saucepan over a medium heat, then add the remaining 1 tablespoon of oil. When it is hot, add the carrot, celery, onion and garlic, then turn the heat to very low. Cover the vegetables with a wet piece of greaseproof paper, cover the pan with a lid and leave them to sweat for 6–8 minutes until they are very tender.

Add the roasted bones to the pan, then pour in the water and add the peppercorns, thyme sprigs, bay leaf and a pinch of salt. Bring to the boil, skimming the surface as necessary. Lower the heat and leave to simmer, partially covered, for 3–4 hours.

Remove and discard the bones, then strain the stock into a large bowl. Leave to cool completely, then cover and chill for up to 4 days. Remove the fat from the surface before using. The stock can also be frozen for up to 4 months.

A

almonds Parma ham, parsley and shallot butter 82–3

anchovies woodcock breakfast 241

apples

apple and chicory salad 180–1

apple and sultana sauce 184–6

poached grouse breast and spelt autumn salad 208

roast crisp pork belly and roasted apples with apple sauce 34

roast pheasant with a cabbage and apple salad 160–1

venison burgers with celeriac soup and fried quail's eggs 75–7

venison tartare and apple with hazelnut mayonnaise 78

whole suckling pig 49

apricots hare terrine 123–5

artichokes

braised stuffed rabbit legs and artichoke and chorizo barigoule 108–10

sautéed lamb sweetbreads and baby artichokes on sourdough toast 55

Asian-flavoured wild duck broth and noodles 260

Asian poached pheasant 164

asparagus

chicken and wild mushroom cream sauce 148–50

pork and prawn patty broth 37

aubergines herb-crusted rack of lamb with ratatouille 59–61

avocado blackened chicken tacos with avocado and pea guacamole 157

B

bacon *see also* lardons; pancetta

hare terrine 123–5

roasted woodcock on toast 238

woodcock breakfast 241

Barnsley chops with a spicy olive relish 65

beans

braised rabbit legs, red pepper and haricot beans 107

chicken confit lollipops and garlic with raw vegetable salad 151–3

crispy chicken and curried spelt salad with raita 142–4

hare, butter bean and chorizo soup 119

oxtail soup with cheese on toast 20–1

pigeon, grape and caramelised walnut salad 222–4

pork and prawn patty broth 37

sautéed lamb sweetbreads and baby artichokes on sourdough toast 55

slow-roast shoulder of lamb with French bean salad 52

wood pigeon breasts with creamed mushrooms in vol-au-vents 225–7

beansprouts pork and prawn patty broth 37

beef

braised and glazed Jacob's ladders 23

onglet steaks with hash browns and fried eggs 27

oxtail soup with cheese on toast 20–1

peppered fillet steaks 28

roast topside with all the trimmings 14–6

roasted bone marrow and girolles with crispy ox tongue 24–5

steak and kidney pie with roasted bone marrow 17–9

T-bone steaks with bone marrow marmalade 31

beef stock 278

beer barbecued beer-can pheasant 177

beetroot

roasted grouse breast and warm roast vegetable salad 200–1

roasted loin of hare with beetroot, celeriac and turnip gratin 116

black pudding ultimate 11s grouse sandwiches 207

blackberries

partridge and game pie with blackberry compôte 187–9

roast rack of venison with a blueberry and juniper crust 72–4

smoked venison loin rolls with celeriac and carrot rémoulade 85

blueberries

poached grouse breast and spelt autumn salad 208

roast rack of venison with a blueberry and juniper crust 72–4

bone marrow

roasted bone marrow and girolles with crispy ox tongue 24–5

steak and kidney pie with roasted bone marrow 17–9

T-bone steaks with bone marrow marmalade 31

braised lamb neck with pea and lettuce ragoût 66–7

bread

grouse and girolle broth with mushroom and liver toasts 212–3

herb-crusted venison livers with shallot reduction on toast 81

open partridge and pancetta toasties with onion compôte 183

oxtail soup with cheese on toast 20–1

partridge breasts and liver pâté on toast 180–1

pigeon, lentil and spelt cheeseburgers 235

pulled pork sandwiches 42–3

roast grouse, game chips and bread sauce 203

roasted woodcock on toast 238

sautéed lamb sweetbreads and baby artichokes on sourdough toast 55

smoked pigeon and poached egg salad 221

ultimate 11s grouse sandwiches 207

woodcock à la ficelle 250

woodcock and pumpkin soup 246–7

broad beans

chicken confit lollipops and garlic with raw vegetable salad 151–3

crispy chicken and curried spelt salad with raita 142–4

pork and prawn patty broth 37

sautéed lamb sweetbreads and baby artichokes on sourdough toast 55

wood pigeon breasts with creamed mushrooms in vol-au-vents 225–7

burgers

pigeon, lentil and spelt cheeseburgers 235

venison burgers with celeriac soup and fried quail's eggs 75–7

butter

clarified 276

About the Author

Tom Kitchin is one of the country's leading chefs, and has been demonstrating his deep-rooted passion, flair and creativity for cooking since he opened his restaurant The Kitchin in Edinburgh, with his wife Michaela in 2006.

The restaurant was quickly awarded a Michelin star in just six months, making Tom Kitchin Scotland's youngest Michelin starred Chef Proprietor at just 29. Tom's culinary CV extends from early training at The Gleneagles Hotel to a decade of working alongside culinary legends including Pierre Koffmann and Alain Ducasse in London and Europe. He has combined his first class training with his passion for innovative, seasonal cooking, and has become synonymous with his 'From Nature to Plate' ethos that runs through the core of his restaurant, championing fresh, seasonal produce, cooked from the heart.

His eponymous restaurant The Kitchin, as well as his award-winning gastro pub, The Scran & Scallie, have both been acknowledged as some of the best places to dine in Britain.

Tom has published two popular books, *From Nature to Plate* and *Kitchin Suppers*, and he has become a well-known face on British television, having appeared on BBC's *Saturday Kitchen* and *The One Show*, as a mentor on *The Chef's Protégé* and as a judge on *Masterchef* Final Chef's Table panel.

Acknowledgements

I would like to sincerely thank everyone who has helped to contribute in the making of this book. It's been a dream come true but I couldn't have done it without some particularly inspirational and important people around me…

Jon Croft from Absolute Press for your encouragement and for inspiring me to take the job on, and to Emily North for all the support shown throughout the project.

Matt Inwood, creative genius.

Pierre Koffmann for teaching me the joy of eating a young grouse. Marc Millar for incredible photos and flexibility around my schedule.

My chefs Craig MacKenzie and Lachlan Archibald for your can-do attitudes and for helping out on your days off. My team at The Kitchin and The Scran & Scallie for helping out and supporting the making of this book.

Holly Napoli for typing recipes and for keeping me right.

Mum and Dad for always showing support. Michaela, my wife and best friend, for your love and for helping me on yet another project. My gorgeous wee boys Kasper, Axel, Logan and Lachlan. I love you.

And last but not least to my incredible suppliers of meat and game as without you guys none of this would be possible.

Publisher Jon Croft
Commissioning Editor Meg Avent
Project Editor Emily North
Art Director and Prop Stylist Matt Inwood
Designers Marie O'Mara and Nathan Shellard
Photographer Marc Millar
Food Stylist Tom Kitchin
Recipe Editor Beverly le Blanc
Proofreader Zoe Ross
Home Economist Elaine Byfield
Indexer Ruth Ellis